THE FAMILY AND THE LAW

THE FAMILY AND THE LAW

SARAH T. KNOX

Chapel Hill

THE UNIVERSITY OF NORTH CAROLINA PRESS

1941

FOREWORD

THE FAMILY AND THE LAW is a book for which there is genuine need. It brings together and states in concise form the legal information which the student of the family and the social worker most often wish to know but which in its original sources is widely scattered and therefore difficult for the lay reader to find quickly and to interpret with confidence.

The author has had the background of personal experience as an administrator of a social agency and of training in the study of law which makes this useful book possible. She writes with clearness, tolerance, and freedom from personal prejudices; and therefore her book reveals that practicality which has had so much to do with her successful career in social administration.

ERNEST R. GROVES

PREFACE

THE following pages have been written with the hope that they will bring to social workers and interested laymen a better understanding of the fundamentals of our legal system, and of the reasons back of its development.

In a general sense there is no division of the law that does not relate to human beings or some aspect of living. Negotiable instruments, corporation law, and insurance—to mention only a few examples—in some way and at some time affect the lives of all of us. Since there had to be a selection and limitation, only those sections of law which affect the family most directly have been considered, for it is in these fields that legal information is of the greatest value to social workers. Though the chapters on criminal law, procedure, and evidence may not seem to affect the family very closely, they were included in order to give some idea of the working mechanics of the law.

Formerly the law was mainly concerned with protecting the life and property rights of the individual, but now it emphasizes new values involving the welfare of human beings in a changing world. The problems which the law has to consider are social, economic, medical, and psychological; they are closely related to those which concern social workers, economists, and physicians. For this reason the law, like other branches of learning, cannot be thought of as self-sufficient; it is one of the interdependent and vital forces which must change to meet new conditions if the communities which it serves are to advance. Life in the decades which developed the common law of England differed from life in the early years in America, and the life of today moves much more rapidly than it did in former days. From the small groups of the household and neighborhood, which were often economically independent, we have developed a complex life in cities where industry and commerce have created various problems. Of necessity legal rules have developed to cope with them. Many people, however, believe that the conditions of modern life call for a more extensive reshaping of legal doctrines and that the law has not met this responsibility.

These pages are designed to create a tolerance born of greater understanding of the law and to further the belief that legal, economic, and social points of view, far from being opposed, are in accord on important issues of mutual concern.

SARAH T. KNOX

CONTENTS

THE FAMILY AND THE LAW

1.

THE DEVELOPMENT OF LAW

ALTHOUGH *law* is a little word it has a significance out of proportion to its size, and its meaning varies with its association. For instance, the law of God, the law of nature, and the law of political economy all mean something quite different from law in its legal application. Law in its legal sense is a rule of conduct which is enforceable by the State through its tribunals or officers.[1] Though this treatise is intended mainly for practical information on the laws which closely affect the family, the brief historical account in the following pages is needed for a clear understanding of various terms and references.

THE LAW OF PRIMITIVE MAN

Primitive man first had to learn to keep himself alive, for self-preservation and self-perpetuation were always the basic laws of nature. Like social animals they lived not

[1] There are many definitions of law but this is a simple one. All writers agree that law is a rule of human conduct. In addition, it has force back of it which is supplied by a governing power.

as individuals but in groups. These progenitors of the human race did not develop the acquisitive instinct very early, as they had no need for it. Property was held by the group, and there was no stealing, no need for contracts, and no possible action arising from an injury to property or a violation of property rights. But gradually certain rules of conduct were approved. Everyone was expected to act according to these rules or be ostracized, and in this way custom crystallized into the general law. Changes later came about when conduct that had been disapproved was accepted or when conduct which had been accepted was disapproved, for law always follows approval or disapproval and, as we find today, cannot go beyond public opinion.

EARLY DEVELOPMENTS TOWARD A LEGAL SYSTEM

The development of law is shown through the history of various civilizations which have tried, in one way or another, to promote justice. The first written expression that has come down to us of a desire to safeguard the welfare of the people and prevent the strong from oppressing the weak is contained in the Code of Hammurabi. This was written upon stone and clay and set forth the rules of conduct in force in Babylon in 2000 B.C. The Hebrews, through their priests as lawgivers, showed the influence of Babylon but went further in their desire for justice. To them righteousness was synonymous with justice, and so moral excellence and responsibility became the basis of their law. In the Commandments, the best known part of Mosaic law, we find precepts which are the basis of our criminal law today, such as the admonition not to kill and not to steal, as well as other regulations that are a pattern for our conduct and are prescribed by social sanctions and legal restrictions.

DEVELOPMENT OF THE ROMAN SYSTEM OF LAW

During a period of a thousand years, from 753 B.C. to 250 A.D., the Romans developed a system of law which was called the Roman or civil law. It is one of the two great systems of unwritten law of the world, as contrasted with written or statute law; the other is the common law of England. Both are very important because the laws of every civilized nation in Europe and America are based upon one or the other of these systems. The Roman system was developed by a process of analysis of individual cases which then became the precedent in subsequent analogous cases. This careful weighing of facts resembled the techniques used in other professions that deal with human problems today, and it carried out the Roman idea of justice, which was "a constant and perpetual willingness to render each one his right."

For about three centuries after the conquest of England, Roman government and civilization flourished there, but when the Romans returned to defend Rome in the fifth century internal struggles began. The Danes and Anglo-Saxons eventually conquered most of what is now England; Roman influence was displaced and Roman law was destroyed, though with various modifications this system was retained throughout Continental Europe. The period of Anglo-Saxon-Danish rule was marked by the growth of a great variety of local customs which were somewhat similar to law and were in force after the Norman Conquest, yet no true body of law was developed at this time.

THE FEUDAL SYSTEM AFTER THE NORMAN CONQUEST

The development of a definite system of law in England dates from the Norman Conquest in 1066, when feudalism was strengthened in its operation. This system had a two-fold purpose; namely, to give protection in time of war and to regulate the economic structure. Taxes and benefits were levied on the people, and an order established in which political rights depended upon land tenure. This was far-reaching in its social effect. William of Normandy, as conqueror of England, through confiscation or surrender came into control of the lands of all who had fought against him. These lands became the property of the Crown and were awarded to the chiefs or barons. The barons in turn granted favors to those under them, but the king was lord paramount and the original owner of all the land in the kingdom. The lord or baron reserved that portion of the manorial land which was necessary for his own use and divided the rest into four parts, according to the type of service he expected from his tenants. Some of the tenants defended the lord against invasion and held their land under military tenure or knight service. Others ploughed the lord's land or returned a certain portion of their crops to him; still others gave services of a personal or religious nature, and in return for all of these services the tenants received protection. Fees were exacted to pay the lord's ransom in case he should be captured, to knight his son, or to provide a marriage dowry for his daughter. Sometimes money was accepted instead of military service. There was a tax corresponding to our inheritance tax and, in very early times, land was inalienable, coming back to the lords on the death of their vassals. Social and legal disputes grew out of these conditions as England gradually developed a legal system.

DEVELOPMENT OF THE COMMON LAW

The common law system of England was based on customs which had become so much a part of the life of the people that they were regarded as a legal force in the community. But in order to have legal recognition the custom must have been in force since time immemorial or, as Blackstone said, "It must have been used so long that the memory of man runneth not to the contrary." Also, it must have been constantly observed and without dispute, consistent with the spirit of the law and with all other customs; certain and not vague, and binding upon all persons. When the law did not provide a rule to govern a case, the judge made the necessary rule, giving consideration to the customs of the community. The courts kept records of the decisions, and it became the practice to consult these in making later decisions. By this method it finally became the rule that the decisions in previous cases should govern when they applied to the facts in question. In time, of course, judicial decisions largely replaced custom as a source of authority.

In a broad sense the term common law is used to contrast the entire system of English law with other systems, such as the Roman or civil law. In its more restricted sense it is used to distinguish the rules of unwritten law which were applied in England by the courts of law as distinguished from Courts of Equity or Ecclesiastical Courts.

The common law influenced the legal development in

this country, for it was adopted by the colonists insofar as it was applicable to conditions in America.[2] It is the basis of our law but changes have been brought about, both by judicial decisions and legislative acts. In the following pages there will be references to the sources which have contributed to our present development, as well as to the modifications which have been developed by a changing family and community life.

COURTS IN ENGLAND

A system of courts administered the common law. After the Norman Conquest the king was considered the fountain of justice; the administration of justice came to be looked upon as his prerogative and was enforced through the Court of the King's Bench (which took its name from the fact that the sovereign was supposed to sit in person), the Court of Common Pleas, and the Court of Exchequer. The Court of the King's Bench had jurisdiction in all criminal cases. The Court of Common Pleas owed its origin to the Magna Charta of 1215 and heard suits between subjects. The king's presence was not necessary. The Court of Exchequer, as its name indicates, was the financial agency of the government and assumed judicial functions in connection with the management of royal revenue.

THE BEGINNING OF THE COURT OF EQUITY

When people wished redress which the common law courts did not give, they made a petition directly to the

---

[2] California, Louisiana, and Texas, which were settled by the French and the Spanish, followed Roman law.

king. However, in time there were too many petitions for the king to consider and they were addressed to the chancellor, who was the king's chief adviser and the keeper of his conscience. Out of this practice the Court of Equity developed. Equity is defined as that branch of jurisprudence which affords a remedy when there is no plain, complete, and adequate remedy at law. It is evident that the English common law did not keep up with the idea of justice of the English people and that it retained the impress of primitive times through many centuries. We can go back to the Roman lawgivers to find a precedent for the system of equity; for while the Romans had no separate courts, they were able to promote and control the entire legal development with equitable principles as the needs of a progressive civilization demanded.

REASONS FOR ITS DEVELOPMENT

Although it is usually said that the Court of Equity was necessary because of the rigidity of the common law, as a matter of fact there were other forces that contributed to its growth. One was the jury system of the common law courts. These courts dealt with only two parties or sets of parties, as complicated cases involving many parties could not be handled by a jury. The relief given in these courts was not always adequate. For example, the common law recognized as the owner of property only the person who had the legal title to it in the form already established by the common law. If A conveyed title of land to B, his son, upon B's promise to allow A the beneficial use of it, B was absolute owner at common law and his promise to A, a moral obligation, was not enforceable. If a party to a valid contract refused to carry out the agreement, the only remedy which the injured party had at law was to sue for damages, which was often an inadequate compensation. For example, if the contract called for a specific house which was of particular value to the buyer, the payment of money would not satisfy him. At common law he could not sue and obtain the particular house, but equity would grant the relief required and order the seller to execute and deliver the deed necessary to pass title, or, in other words, would grant specific performance of the contract.

GRADUAL PROGRESS TO A DEFINITE SYSTEM

At first the Chancellor decided all cases in accordance with his own idea of equity, which meant that he was not administering any particular system of law. Following this there grew up the practice of looking at previous decisions in similar cases, as the common law courts had done, and principles were worked out which formed a basis for a system of rules for this court. Finally certain maxims of equity evolved and these are the foundation upon which equity jurisprudence has been based. While they are not the final principles and rules, they are the beginnings from which the rules have developed. A brief explanation of some of these maxims will establish their importance.

THE MAXIMS OF EQUITY

Perhaps the most important maxim is: equity regards that as done which ought to be done—not what might be done, but what in good conscience should be done; and another maxim explains that it does this by looking at the intent of the parties rather than the form in which the intent is shown. These maxims act with and aid each other and are the foundation of all equitable property rights as distinguished from legal ownership. The maxim that equity will regard that as done which ought to be done is important, for it relates to the contracts of individuals, to deeds, and to the theory of uses and trusts which we shall see later became of great importance to women and their property rights.

There is a very early case of Lady A, who, without joining her husband, sued her father-in-law to obtain specific performance of a certain covenant in her favor in the deed of settlement made upon her marriage. This would not have been possible at common law, and it shows the two most important functions of equity jurisprudence then known—the protection of the wife's separate estate and specific performance of a contract.[8]

Equity assists only the person who has a just claim. As expressed by the two familiar maxims, "He who seeks equity must do equity" and "One must come into court with clean hands." This means that if there is anything that should be done by the person asking for the remedy he must be prepared to do it before expecting relief. There must be no iniquitous conduct in relation to the transaction in question. For example, a gambling debt would not be enforceable. It is the same principle which applies in divorce cases: if the one seeking release has been guilty of misconduct, a divorce will not be granted.

THE FUNCTION OF EQUITY

Some of the maxims refer to the manner of carrying out the principles which form the structure upon which

---

[8] Sir F. Palgrave, *History of the Council*, pp. 64–67.

equity is based. Before leaving this subject it should be emphasized that the rules of equity are not rigid. They are based upon the principles of justice, right, and duty as applied to the events and doings of society. These principles are applied by the courts to legal relations and have been made to assume a legal character without losing their essential ethical force.

The Court of Equity in England existed as a separate tribunal for many centuries, but it finally disappeared there as it has in most of the states in this country.[4] Today the lines which divided common law and equity have been removed and though the rules of procedure and remedies are still kept separate the same court usually acts as a court of law and a court of equity, and the same judge enforces both legal and equitable remedies.

[4] Separate Courts of Equity exist in Alabama, Delaware, Mississippi, New Jersey, and Tennessee, but even these states have only one appellate tribunal of last resort.

2.

LEGAL RIGHTS AND WRONGS

THE development of legal systems brought a recognition of certain rights belonging to individuals who live together in society, and of corresponding wrongs when these rights are violated. The rights, which represent some power, interest, or privilege which the law will enforce, are either absolute or relative. In the first group are the rights of personal security, of personal liberty, and of private property. These are fundamental rights which nations, through the centuries, have struggled to obtain and to maintain. They have been stated in various documents in both England and this country from the time of the Magna Charta in 1215 and the Bill of Rights in 1689 to our own Declaration of Independence and the Constitution of the United States.

THE RIGHT OF PERSONAL SECURITY

The right of personal security is the right of freedom from injury to life, limb, body, health, or reputation. Law and society recognize a man's natural right to live, even though he has conducted himself in a way which makes him a menace to the welfare of society. However, his right of freedom is then subordinated to the welfare of the whole group. For the purpose of legal interpretation, it should be explained that at common law the members of the body were those parts which were useful in fighting and included not only the arms and legs but eyes, front teeth, and any other parts needed for self-defense. Loss of an ear or nose was not included, for this did not weaken the fighting power. The offense of cutting off some part was called *mayhem* at common law, but it is now generally treated as assault. A person has the right to defend himself when his life is in danger, even to the point of taking life when it is necessary for his own protection.

An individual's right of personal security may be affected in other ways, and the law recognizes that everyone has the right of immunity from injury to health and reputation. When a person is given poisonous food or his reputation is attacked in writing (libel) or in speech (slander), a right is violated and there is a legal remedy. The term for a wrong of this character is *tort;* and the wrong may be so serious that the state will consider it a crime and will punish the offender.

THE RIGHT OF PERSONAL LIBERTY

The right of personal liberty gives an individual the right to act with freedom unless the particular act is restricted by law. Freedom of speech, for example, does not give one the right to use libelous or slanderous language against another person. Freedom of moral action likewise is restricted, for we have definite legal rules that prescribe conduct in relation to society, regardless of any personal views which the individual may hold.

THE RIGHT OF PRIVATE PROPERTY

This is the right to own and possess property and is the third fundamental right. Ownership and possession are quite different and the distinction is important for an understanding of the rights that are involved. If a person owns property, he has the right of absolute control over it; he can lease, sell, or make contracts concerning it, unless the law places some restriction on him. Possession, on the contrary, means holding the property only, and may be rightful or in violation of the owner's rights. Possession of property permits a person to hold it against anyone except the true owner, however, which probably accounts for the saying that possession is nine points of the law.

The right to own property has seemed almost as important to man as life itself. The Jewish people considered it so important that marriage outside the tribe was forbidden. A widow could call upon her deceased husband's nearest male relative to marry her; her land came to him through the marriage. Under certain systems of government, property is held in common instead of by individuals; as one looks about the world today one wonders how long the right to hold property will be an inalienable right of man.

THE PROTECTION OF ABSOLUTE RIGHTS

The first concern of the law was the protection of the absolute rights of individuals, which have been discussed above. Therefore the law of crimes, which controls the penalties imposed by the state for injuries to persons and property, and the law of torts, which determines the civil liability for injuries and wrongs to persons and property, developed before the law of contracts. The latter is based upon the rights and obligations imposed by the will of the parties, or those agreements which are implied in law because of the circumstances.

The law of contracts developed very slowly up to the time of the Norman Conquest but commerce, which had become stabilized as a result of security to persons and property, brought about the necessity for agreements which would be enforceable.

CONTRACTS

The law of contracts controls many of the acts and relationships of our daily lives. Insurance policies and negotiable instruments are common examples of contracts, and partnership, mercantile transactions, agency, suretyship, and the renting of property are all governed by contracts of one form or another. So many fields of the law are involved that a knowledge of the subject is important.

The shortest definition of a contract is "an agreement or promise enforceable at law." There are many agreements not enforceable at law, for instance, a social agreement to accept an invitation to dinner. There are six essentials in a valid contract and these will be discussed briefly, though it is not advisable to consider the variations and exceptions that can center around each of these, sometimes making the construction, operation, and discharge of the contract obligation a fine point of legal interpretation.

Offer and Acceptance.— The term *agreement* implies that there are at least two parties involved, and, further, that one party proposes something and the other agrees. Hence it is reducible to offer and acceptance. Both parties must intend the same thing or, in legal terms, there must be a meeting of the minds. The offer may be made in various ways and the acceptance by giving a promise or performing an act. To take a common illustration, a street car is a constant offer to the public to ride and when a person steps into the car he accepts the offer and pays the fare. There are many rules that govern offer and acceptance.

Consideration.— Consideration is defined as some right, interest, profit, or benefit accruing to one party, or some detriment, loss, or responsibility given, suffered, or undertaken by the other party.[1] There must be consideration to support a simple contract. If A promises to work for B for twenty dollars a month, there is good consideration and a valid contract. Consideration need not be money but may be something of value given in exchange for a promise. For example, a promise to pay another person a sum of money if he would abstain from the use of liquor and tobacco for a given time was considered binding when the party did abstain, for he had a legal right to use liquor and tobacco and his abstinence was a surrender of that right.[2]

Legal Form.— Contracts must be in the form prescribed by law. Deeds and some formal contracts require a seal,

---

[1] W. L. Clark, *Contracts*, Sections 61–62.

[2] Homer v. Sidway, 124 N. Y. 538.

in which case no express consideration is needed, for the seal is presumed to be conclusive evidence of consideration.

Competent Parties.— The parties must have the capacity to enter into a legal agreement. In general there are two classes that are incapable of making contracts except as to necessaries:

1. Those who lack mental capacity, such as insane persons and those who are so intoxicated that they are unable to understand what they are doing.

2. Those who have mental capacity but lack legal capacity, such as infants under twenty-one, and, formerly, both married women and aliens.

Corporations are artificial persons created by law, and they have a limited power to contract.

The Consent Must Be Genuine.— The mutual consent which is essential to every contract must be real. If there is no real consent because of mistake, misrepresentation, fraud, duress, or undue influence, there is no contract because the parties did not agree on the same thing.

Legal Subject Matter.— The subject matter of the contract must be legal, otherwise the contract will not be legal even though all other elements are present. Illegal contracts include agreements to do an act prohibited by law, or one that is contrary to public policy. Agreements to carry on the sale of liquor when this is contrary to statutory prohibition, or to obstruct justice by preventing a criminal prosecution are examples of illegal contracts.

FURTHER PROVISION IN PARTICULAR CONTRACTS

The Statute of Frauds, which was enacted in England in 1676 to prevent fraudulent acts, is followed in this country and relates to certain contracts which must be in writing and be signed by the parties in order to be valid.[8] These include agreements relating to the liability of an executor or administrator to answer for damages out of his own estate; contracts concerning real estate; agreements to answer for the debt of another; agreements made in consideration of marriage; agreements not to be performed within a year; and contracts for the sale of goods over a certain sum unless the goods have been received or unless partial payment has been made on them.

A contract obligation is either performed as agreed or there is failure to perform, which constitutes a breach. The injured party has a remedy, which is to go into court and recover damages or, as has been stated, equity may

---

[8] The fourth and seventeenth sections of the original Statute of Frauds are as follows:

The Fourth Section.—

"No action shall be brought whereby to charge any executor or administrator upon any special promise to answer damages out of his own estate; or whereby to charge the defendant upon any special promise to answer for the debt, default, or miscarriages of another person; or to charge any person upon any agreement made upon consideration of marriage; or upon any contract or sale of lands, tenements, or hereditaments, or any interest in or concerning them; or upon any agreement that is not to be performed within the space of one year from the making thereof; unless the agreement upon which such action shall be brought, or some memorandum or note thereof, shall be in writing, and signed by the party to be charged therewith, or some other person thereunto by him lawfully authorized."

The Seventeenth Section.—

"No contract for the sale of any goods, wares, or merchandises for the price of £10 sterling, or upwards, shall be allowed to be good, except the buyer shall accept part of the goods so sold, and actually receive the same, or give something in earnest to bind the bargain, or in part payment, or that some note or memorandum in writing of the said bargain be made and signed by the parties to be charged by such contract, or their agents thereunto lawfully authorized."

grant him the specific terms of the contract. If the relief is in money, the court will award only the amount which will put the injured party in as good position as he would have been if the other party had kept his promise.

3.

LEGAL MACHINERY FOR SETTLING DISAGREEMENTS

LEGAL machinery to settle disputes is necessary, and courts have been substituted for the early methods of trial which were very crude. In England trials by oath, by ordeal, and by battle were expected to give redress and to establish justice. The first was not based on the oath of a witness that he had personal knowledge of certain facts, but depended on the testimony of a number of people who swore that they believed the person guilty or innocent.

Trial by ordeal would seem to us an even more impossible method of determining justice. The accused was forced to take a red hot iron in his hand, or to plunge his arm in boiling water, or to be thrown into cold water. If he was not affected by the hot iron or water or could swim in cold water, he was innocent; otherwise, he was declared guilty. These two means of settling disagreements were used chiefly in criminal cases.

Trial by battle was fought with cudgels in the presence

of a judge, and if neither of the parties was overcome continued from sunrise until night. This method of trial was practiced to some extent in England until 1819. Now disputes are settled in court by a trial before a judge, or before a judge and jury.

THE EARLY JURY

One development of the English law which was different from other systems was the trial by jury, but the original jury was not like the jury of today. It consisted of an indefinite number of men who were chosen because they already knew something about the cause at issue and merely reported this knowledge. It was many centuries before the jury came to be what it is today; namely, a body of twelve men who must give a unanimous verdict based upon the evidence presented to them by witnesses, who are under oath to give true testimony. The admissibility of evidence is regulated by rules, and the counsel for the respective litigants largely control the modern trial.

The term *court* like the word *law* has more than one meaning. Blackstone defined a court as a place where justice is judicially administered; but when reference is made to the jurisdiction of the court or the decision of the court it is clearly applicable to the judge who is acting in his official capacity, and refers to a person rather than a place.

JURISDICTION

A court has either original or appellate jurisdiction, depending upon whether it has the power to hear and determine controversies in the first instance or upon appeal to review and correct the decision of an inferior court. A court also has general or limited jurisdiction. If it has general jurisdiction, it has the power to decide all controversies; but if the jurisdiction is limited, it can decide controversies of a particular class only. Courts which have to do with the settling of estates are an example of limited jurisdiction.

SOURCES OF FEDERAL AND STATE LAWS

The Federal Government and each of the forty-eight states have a complete system of courts. The written law of the Federal Government consists of the Federal Constitution, the treaties made by its authority, and the acts of Congress. The written law of the individual state consists of the state constitution and the statutes enacted by the state legislature.

JUDICIAL POWER PLACED IN THE SUPREME COURT

The Constitution of the United States provides that "the judicial power of the United States shall be vested in one Supreme Court, and in such inferior courts as the Congress may from time to time ordain and establish." [1] The Supreme Court has original jurisdiction in cases affecting certain representatives of the Government and cases in which a state is a party against another state. In all other cases its jurisdiction is appellate. Its function is most important, as it carries the responsibility of finality in important and far-reaching decisions.

---

[1] Article III, Sec. 2.

OTHER FEDERAL COURTS [2]

Next in order of importance is the United States Circuit Court of Appeals. The judicial districts of the United States are divided by groups of states into nine circuits, and in each of the nine circuits there is a court called the Circuit Court of Appeals, which hears appeals from the decision of the district courts. Each of the nine circuits is divided into districts and in each district there is a district court. Sometimes a state constitutes a single district, while other states contain two or more districts. The district courts exercise the larger part of the original jurisdiction vested in the judicial department of the Federal Government. There is a Court of Claims which was established to determine claims of individuals against the United States Government; also a Court of Customs Appeals and a Commerce Court, both of which have jurisdiction over special classes of federal cases.

STATE COURTS

The systems of courts in the various states differ greatly from each other but have some general features in common. In all states there is a court of final appeal, which may be the Supreme Court or the Court of Appeals. In some states there are courts of intermediate appeal as well. There are courts of general original jurisdiction, courts of inferior original jurisdiction, and courts of special probate jurisdiction. The courts of general original jurisdiction are usually called circuit courts, district courts, courts of common pleas, or superior courts; and

[2] 25 C. J., pp. 685–1007.

the inferior courts, which have limited jurisdiction in civil and criminal matters, are called by a variety of names—justice courts, police courts, magistrates' courts, etc. The court of special probate jurisdiction, which usually has to do with guardianships and adoptions, as well as with estates, is ordinarily called the probate court but in some states is called the orphans' court or the surrogate court.

SPECIAL COURTS

The two special courts which have the most to do with family relationships are the juvenile court and the court of domestic relations. They are the most recent developments in legal procedure and show the present trend toward social legislation.

Every state has developed some form of a juvenile court for children's cases. The jurisdiction includes the group of children known as neglected, dependent and delinquent.

The courts of domestic relations or family courts, as the name indicates, have to do with the various difficulties and relationships of the family. The jurisdiction varies even in these courts, but in those having the widest scope it includes divorce, non-support, adoption, guardianship, and crimes against children. In some states it also includes the function of the juvenile court, thereby embracing in its jurisdiction every action which affects the family.

FAMILY CONFLICTS

There is an advantage in bringing all controversies which have to do with the family into one court, with the records centered in one place. This seems a logical procedure to avoid the confusion that results in many states, when divorces may come under the jurisdiction of one court, action for non-support be brought in a different court, and guardianship or other actions affecting the child come before still another tribunal.

4.

MARRIAGE AND DIVORCE

THE author of *The Family and Social Work* says: "Our modern monogamous family represents the survival of religious, ethical, economic, and legal elements from all the intermingling streams which unite to make the civilization of which it is a part. Hebrew, Roman, Teuton, and others more remote have made their contribution." [1]

Recent writers stress the importance of the family in a different way: "People do not marry because it is their social duty to perpetuate the institution of the family, or because the preacher and Mrs. Grundy both recommend matrimony, or even because they fall in love with each other. They marry because they lived in a family as children and still cannot get over the feeling that being in a family is the only proper, indeed the only possible, way to live." [2]

The normal conventional family starts with marriage, but the history of this institution shows that it has taken centuries to develop to its present rank in the social order.

---

[1] Edward T. Devine, *The Family and Social Work*, p. 34.

[2] John Levy and Ruth Munroe, *The Happy Family*, p. 1.

In the early stages of civilization marriage by capture was a favorite method and, as we know, was practised by the Romans. In many countries marriage was not confined to the union of one man and one woman, and polyandry and polygamy were the usual practices. If we agree that the family is the fundamental unit of society and one of the fine developments of civilization we should then examine its status, obligations, and duties from a legal standpoint.

MARRIAGE A CONTRACTUAL RELATIONSHIP

Marriage is commonly said to be a civil contract, but more truly the betrothal or engagement leading up to the marriage is the contract. The marriage grows out of this and when consummated by the legal ceremony and the parties become man and wife, it establishes a legal status which imposes certain rights and privileges as well as obligations. It resembles other contracts because the parties who wish to enter the marriage relation must be legally competent, there must be mutual consent, and the marriage must be in the form prescribed by law. Unlike ordinary contracts which can be set aside if the parties wish, this one cannot be dissolved at the will of the parties because it is of public concern. Formerly it was necessary for the legislature to grant dissolution, but now it is accomplished through the court by a divorce decree. There is another difference in the marriage contract; in practically all other instances the parties must have reached the age of majority in order to make a binding contract but a marriage contract can be made earlier.

There are several limitations which the law places

on those who wish to marry, such as that of age, of near relationship, and of previous marriage even though there is mutual consent and solemnization in the prescribed manner.

THE AGE LIMITATION

At common law a female could marry at twelve and a male at fourteen. This is still the law unless changed by statute but most states have fixed the minimum age, which may be from fourteen to sixteen for females and from seventeen to twenty-one for males. Until very recent years, however, there were eleven states that permitted the marriage of females of twelve years, either by direct provision in the statutes or by lack of any statutory provision, so that the common law prevailed. In most states the minimum age requirement may be waived if the parents consent to it and marriage seems expedient. Pregnancy is often considered a sufficient cause for the waiver, but the policy of granting a license for this reason has questionable value though it seems to settle the problem for the moment and does what so many people think desirable—it gives the baby a name. Social workers, however, know that the emotional wreckage following a marriage under these conditions may be very costly to the individual and to society, and it is often better for the mother to assume the responsibility alone.

CRIMINAL LIABILITY INVOLVED

The criminal factor is often involved, too, if the girl is under the age of consent—the age fixed by statute under which she is presumed to be too young to have consented to sexual intercourse. This age in most states is sixteen. Her pregnancy is therefore the result of a criminal act, for which the man is liable and can be prosecuted. If a marriage takes place it will be a bar to the prosecution for the sex offense in most states, but marriage under these conditions does not provide a good foundation on which to build a satisfactory life.

VOID OR VOIDABLE MARRIAGE AND ANNULMENT

Though there may have been a ceremony, a legal marriage is not always established and as a result the marriage may be void or voidable. If it is void no marriage exists, but if it is voidable and the parties wish to have it set aside legal action must be taken for annulment. Some of the causes which will render a marriage voidable are infancy, the use of force or duress, or fraud which amounts to a false representation, as the concealment of a disease or an untrue statement relating to pregnancy which is material to the marriage relation. A Massachusetts court annulled a marriage on the proof that when the marriage took place the man had a communicable disease. His wife was told of this a short time after the ceremony and before she lived with him. As this affected their marital relations—her health and the health of any children that might be born—the marriage was annulled.[8]

A marriage under the statutory age is usually voidable and not void even if the legal requirements are not met —for instance, if only the parents' consent is obtained when permission from the court is required also, as in New Hampshire. Such marriages as a practical matter are not avoided, for if the parents were willing for the mar-

---

[8] Smith v. Smith, 171 Mass. 404.

riage to take place they clearly will not petition for annulment. One court has held that the parents did not have this right exclusively.[4] A child of thirteen years and seven months was married in New York State and when she was sixteen, as she had not lived with her husband, her father brought action to have the marriage declared void. The court said that the marriage contracts of infants are not dependent upon the parents' consent to the marriage and the parents could not have the marriage annulled on that ground, and further added that it was only the infant wife who could bring the action for annulment.

A very unfortunate situation may arise in a marriage under the statutory age, for if either party wishes to disaffirm the marriage when the minor becomes of age, it is possible to do so and claim that there was no legal marriage, and if there have been children they are illegitimate. On the other hand, the Supreme Court of Ohio held the marriage for nonage invalid unless the parties lived together after arriving at the statutory age. As a rule the courts recognize a legal presumption in favor of marriage because it seems the best public policy and gives protection to women and children.

There must be mutual assent of the parties in order to constitute a marriage and if both parties are in high spirits from imbibing and consider the matter a joke, even though there is a ceremony no marriage exists because the intent is lacking. Also, extreme intoxication which will prevent intelligent action will render a marriage void or voidable, depending upon the statutes. In the absence of statute, according to Tiffany, such marriages are void, but usually by statute they are voidable only.

[4] Wood v. Baker, 88 New York 854.

OTHER IMPEDIMENTS TO MARRIAGE

Consanguinity.— At common law marriage within certain degrees of relationship was prohibited. The disqualifications of relationship were determined by the Church, and the law as enacted in England during the reign of Henry VIII prohibited the marriage of those of nearer relationship than cousins.[5] This ecclesiastical law is followed closely in every state today, and some states prohibit the marriage of first cousins. This prohibitory law was on the ground of the sanctity of the home and the protection of children, for as civilization has advanced people have held incestuous marriage in abhorrence though this was common among Egyptian people.[6]

In South Carolina a man married his niece, a brother's daughter, and when he died action was brought by his children of a former marriage to claim all of the estate on the ground that the marriage with the niece was void

---

[5] A woman may not marry her:	A man may not marry his:
1. Grandfather	1. Grandmother
2. Grandmother's husband	2. Grandfather's wife
3. Husband's grandfather	3. Wife's grandmother
4. Father's brother	4. Father's sister
5. Mother's brother	5. Mother's sister
6. Father's sister's husband	6. Father's brother's wife
7. Mother's sister's husband	7. Mother's brother's wife
8. Husband's father's brother	8. Wife's father's sister
9. Husband's mother's brother.	9. Wife's mother's sister
10. Father	10. Mother
11. Stepfather	11. Stepmother
12. Husband's father	12. Wife's mother
13. Son	13. Daughter
14. Husband's son	14. Wife's daughter

[6] The ancestry of the famous Cleopatra shows the highest inbreeding in recorded history, without ill results. The family furnished illustrious and able rulers for centuries. Cleopatra herself was the child of a brother and sister, and many similar brother-and-sister and uncle-and-niece marriages took place among the relatives.

and that she was not entitled to any of the estate.[7] This court held that a marriage within the prohibited degrees of relationship was not void but voidable and if not dissolved during the lifetime of the parties conferred civil rights of marriage, such as the wife's right of dower in her husband's property.

A New Hampshire decision was in direct opposition to this, for when two cousins married the husband was denied any rights in his wife's property after her death because the statute in force at the time of the marriage prohibited the marriage of first cousins, declaring such a marriage void and the issue of the marriage illegitimate.[8]

Feeblemindedness.— Many states now have statutes prohibiting the marriage of feebleminded persons, and sometimes there is a penalty attached for the one who issues a license to the same. This shows progress and the acknowledgment by public opinion that the State has the right to prohibit marriages which will perpetuate the unfit. However, some legal machinery is needed to aid the official in determining the mental status of the applicant before the law can be wholly effective in preventing such marriages. Some states require the registration of all feebleminded persons and this provides a basis for refusing the license. It is possible to bring an action to nullify such a marriage, and as long ago as 1850 there was a well-known case in New Hampshire.[9] In this instance a girl over twenty-one went into the State of Vermont and was secretly married to a man who probably knew that she had some property. In the petition for annulment

---

[7] Bowers v. Bowers, Court of Errors of S. C., 1858. 10 Rich Equity, 551.

[8] Colbath v. Rollins, 68 N. H. 191.

[9] True v. Ranny, 21 N. H. 52.

her father showed that she could not dress herself, and though she went to the district school until she was twenty she could not spell, add and subtract, or tell the time of day. She could not learn to do housework, and had no idea of the time involved in getting a simple meal; she could neither distinguish colors, count beyond twenty, nor do an errand. She was satisfied to play with toys and with children four or five years of age. It would not seem necessary that the court should be endowed with high intelligence in order to decide that she was entirely incapable of understanding the nature and obligations of marriage.

Insanity.— The question of the marriage of an insane person has never been well settled, and the degree of mental incapacity which will render a marriage invalid is still an open question though it is settled that the mental disease must exist at the time of the marriage. Some authorities hold that insanity renders a marriage voidable and not void if the person temporarily regains reason and affirms the marriage. In most states insanity is not a sufficient ground for divorce, as it would be regarded as harsh for a man to put away his wife because she had become insane. But some types of insanity, being hereditary, go to the very root of the marriage relationship. Probably in time, when there is a better understanding and acknowledgment of mental ills, provision will be made for the protection of future generations through laws prohibiting marriage of the insane and a greater number of states will grant divorce for this reason.

Miscegnation.— On the ground of public policy and for the protection of future generations, miscegnation or the intermarriage of persons of different races—as between Negroes and whites or Indians and whites or Chinese and whites—is prohibited in some southern and western states. There is no prohibitory law in states where the population is largely white, as such legislation has probably never seemed necessary. In some states such a marriage is not only prohibited but may be prosecuted as a crime.

Prior Marriages.— Bigamous marriage has always been prohibited in Christian lands. It was originally an ecclesiastical offense and its prohibition became a part of the common law. Bigamous marriages are usually held to be absolutely void, even though the parties acted in good faith and thought they were free to marry.[10] Any marriage is illegal while a prior marriage is still in force; but if M marries A, and while she is still his wife he marries B, and after the death of A he marries C, the last marriage is not bigamous because the marriage to B was void and upon the death of A he was free to marry. Bigamous marriage, however, brings us into the realm of criminal law.

THE COMMON LAW MARRIAGE

In England a common law marriage was recognized. When two people showed by mutual consent a desire to assume the marriage relationship, living together as husband and wife and having that reputation in the community, no marriage ceremony was held necessary. Court decisions in this country have not been uniform with regard to common law marriages. Many states appear to recognize them, but a court decision may be contrary to the statutory provision; so it is almost impossible to be exact on this point. In Illinois, Mississippi, and New

[10] Chamberlain v. Chamberlain, 68 N. J., Eq. 414.

York a common law marriage is definitely declared not valid, and Arizona, California, Connecticut, Kansas, Louisiana, Utah, Virginia, West Virginia, and Wisconsin affirm that a marriage cannot take place without a license.

At any rate, there must be an intent of the parties to consider themselves married in the eyes of God, and it cannot be merely a casual arrangement nor an agreement to sexual intimacy following a promise of future marriage. This is an unlawful contract, as it is against public morals and is not recognized by the courts.

In many states the question of inheritance of property has been involved with the legality of a common law marriage. In a Minnesota case a man who was supposed to be a bachelor died, leaving a will which he had made many years prior to his death.[11] After the will was proved and probated a former housekeeper of his came forward and stated that she was his wife and asked for the property to which she was entitled by law. To prove this she produced a contract: "Contract of marriage between N. Hulett and Mrs. L. A. Pomroy. Believing a marriage by contract to be perfectly lawful, we do hereby agree to be husband and wife, and to hereafter live together as such." This was signed and sealed by the parties. The court held that though the arrangement was secret and there was no reputation of their marriage in the community, their consent legally expressed made this a marriage and she was entitled to the property.

STATUTORY REQUIREMENTS

The marriage laws of the various states are not uniform but in all jurisdictions there are statutory provisions

[11] Hulett v. Carey, 66 Minn. 327.

which regulate the procedure. These regulations provide for the formalities of obtaining a license or of publishing banns and solemnizing the marriage.

Each year additional states require that a certificate showing that the parties are free from certain communicable diseases must accompany the application for the license. In order that the marriage may not be hasty, many states require an interval of a few days between the application and the granting of the license. The ceremony must be performed by a legally authorized person, either a magistrate, clergyman, priest, or rabbi. The provisions are usually directory instead of mandatory, and a marriage will not be invalid if all the formalities are not obeyed. The final step is the return of the license to the proper officials with the report that the marriage has taken place; this report then becomes a matter of public record and can be verified at any time.

THE LAW OF THE PLACE OF THE MARRIAGE CONTROLS ITS VALIDITY

As with any other contract, the general rule is that a marriage is valid in any state if it is valid where it took place. Some states make an exception to this rule when there is an interlocutory decree of divorce which prohibits another marriage for a certain period of time, and there is a deliberate attempt by both parties to evade the law of the state of their domicile by going into another state in order to marry. Wisconsin, North Carolina, and Tennessee do not recognize this as a valid marriage nor the children of such union as legitimate, while Vermont, New York, and California hold that marriage is prohibited only in the state where the divorce was obtained, and that a marriage outside of that state, even though within the prohibited time, will be recognized in the state where the divorce was granted. This would seem to be a better rule when children are involved.

A SUIT FOR BREACH OF PROMISE TO MARRY

When there is an engagement or a contract to marry and one of the parties refuses to carry out the agreement, the other party can bring a suit for breach of promise. It is usually the woman who brings such a suit and the agreement is proved by evidence which will show the conduct of the offending party.

The only remedy is damages. The financial and social standing of the parties will be taken into consideration, and compensation may be awarded for the pain and injured feelings as well as for loss of time and expense in preparing for marriage. On the other hand, it may not be possible to show that the woman suffered any injury and then she cannot receive damages. Today the trend is to discourage such suits.

DIVORCE AND SEPARATION

Probably no subject has been more generally discussed in recent years than divorce. Its various causes, especially those related to economic insecurity and sexual or emotional incompatibility, have been discussed freely in the press and literature of the day. How they all fit into the legal pigeonholes is another side of the situation.

KINDS OF DIVORCE

Divorce is the legal separation of husband and wife by the judgment of a court. At common law there were two kinds of divorce: *a mensa et thoro* or from bed and board, a qualified divorce which did not dissolve the marriage, and *a vinculo matrimonii* or absolute divorce which dissolved the marriage. In some states a legal separation similar to a divorce *a mensa et thoro* will be granted for certain causes which are not sufficient to justify an absolute divorce, or to couples who do not wish to live together but do not believe in divorce. The parties themselves may enter into an agreement to separate if the separation follows immediately, but they may not agree to separate in the future.

THE QUESTION OF UNIFORMITY

Whether or not we agree with those people who think there should be uniform divorce laws for the entire country, the present situation is undoubtedly confusing. As long as the laws and interpretations regarding the grounds for divorce are different in the various states, a person may find divorce harder to obtain than is generally supposed. Because of this confusion a person may be divorced in one state and still legally bound in another. This was true in a New York case which was finally decided by the United States Supreme Court, this court taking jurisdiction on an appeal, as the suit involved citizens of different states.[12] The matrimonial domicile of the parties was New York. The husband abandoned his wife without just cause and established a new domicile in Connecticut, where he brought suit and obtained a divorce according to the laws of that state. His wife did not appear to contest the suit, but she later brought suit in New York and obtained a decree and alimony. The New York court held that under the law of

[12] Haddock v. Haddock, 201 U. S. 562.

New York that court was not required to note or give effect to the decree of Connecticut. The Supreme Court also refused to require the State of New York to recognize the decree if the husband was guilty of wrongful abandonment. Most states, however, recognize the right of the parties to acquire a new domicile, which means that the court where the new domicile is acquired has jurisdiction and can grant a decree which other states will respect. In this particular case after the Connecticut decree and before the New York decree the man was single in Connecticut while in New York he was still married to his first wife and could not lawfully marry a second time.

GROUNDS FOR DIVORCE

Adultery is the most common legal cause for divorce and all the states except South Carolina, which recognizes no ground for divorce, will grant it on proof of this allegation. In New York State this is the only cause allowed, but in some other states as many as thirteen legal grounds for divorce are recognized. Many of these are closely linked together, and the principal ones are adultery, cruelty, desertion, and non-support. Impotency, habitual drunkenness, conviction of a crime followed by imprisonment, and other miscellaneous causes are recognized less frequently.

Adultery.— Adultery is generally defined as the voluntary sexual intercourse of a married person with a person other than the offender's wife or husband.[18] The various statutes may qualify this definition somewhat. Sometimes one party may suppose the other party to a marriage is

[18] W. L. Clark, *An Analytical Summary of American Law.*

dead and may marry, only to find out later that the supposition was untrue. In such a case some courts consider that no adultery was committed, proceeding upon the theory that to constitute a ground for divorce the same criminal intent is necessary that is required to constitute the crime of adultery or bigamy. The criminal intent is denied by the honest though untrue belief. If there is negligence in not getting the true facts this will not be a defense, for it is looked upon as a mistake of law, and ignorance of the law is no excuse. When a woman was advised by a justice of the peace that she had obtained a divorce and could marry again while in fact the divorce was not legal, she was guilty of adultery when she lived with the one she supposed was her second husband.[14]

Cruelty.— The statutes recognize three types of cruelty. They are cruelty, extreme cruelty, and extreme and repeated cruelty. To constitute cruelty "there must be an infliction or threatened infliction of bodily harm, or words or conduct that cause great mental suffering and thereby injure or threaten to injure the health." Formerly the decisions largely upheld the opinion that there must be physical violence, either actual or threatened, and that mental suffering such as would be caused by a husband accusing his wife of infidelity before their adopted son would not constitute cruelty.[15] Courts of many states now recognize that great mental suffering affects the bodily health and have granted divorce for that as well as for physical cruelty.

Desertion.— The statutory period of time which must elapse before a divorce can be obtained on the grounds of desertion varies from one to five years. To constitute

---

[14] State v. Goodenow, 65 Me. 30.

[15] Mathewson v. Mathewson, 81 Vt. 173.

desertion there must be an actual cessation of cohabitation for the entire statutory period. There must be an intent to desert without the consent of the other party and there must be no misconduct which would justify the abandonment. Probably wives are deserted more often than husbands even though the law recognizes the husband's right to pick out the domicile and the wife's duty to follow her husband. If she fails to do so she is guilty of desertion. Refusal to emigrate from England to America was considered desertion by one court, but an Illinois court decreed that failure to live in the home of a mother-in-law was not desertion. A separation for business reasons or illness will not constitute desertion, but if after being apart for some time one party develops an intent to desert, the required statutory period will date from the time the intent is formed.

An offer to return to the domicile of the husband or wife within the required period will bar desertion as a ground for divorce. A husband is not obliged to support his wife away from his domicile, but if his conduct is such that she is driven away and he is able but does not support her this amounts to desertion. According to decisions in several states, it makes no difference whether the husband deserts his wife or so conducts himself that she is forced to leave him.[16]

Non-Support.— Some statutes combine non-support and desertion, but non-support alone may be a ground for divorce. Non-support is a relative condition and the court will take into consideration the station in life of the parties. The person—usually the wife—is entitled to sufficient support to enable her to live according to the

---

[16] James v. James, 58 N. H. 266; Wood v. Wood, 27 N. C. 674; Almond v. Almond, 25 Va. 662, all hold this view.

standard of life to which she is accustomed. This includes such necessities as food and clothing, and may even include jewels and furniture. If the husband is not able to support his wife, a divorce will not be granted for non-support, according to a decision in Texas.

Habitual Drunkenness.— In order to obtain a divorce for drunkenness this must be confirmed and habitual—merely occasional imbibing is not enough.

Conviction of a Crime.— Conviction of a crime which amounts to a felony and is followed by a sentence to the state prison for two years or more is a ground for divorce in some states. There has been some question as to whether a pardon would destroy the right of divorce action, but the general rule is that it does not and this is expressly stated in the statutes of some states. A few states even provide by statute that the conviction of certain crimes shall work a dissolution of the marriage without legal process.

WIDE PROVISIONS FOR DIVORCE

Public sentiment increasingly concurs in the belief that if two people cannot get along together their marriage should be dissolved, and some states have made sweeping provisions for divorce for any reason which has made married life a failure. Some people even go so far as to advocate that if mutual consent is necessary to bring about a marriage it should work just as well the other way, and if two people have agreed that they cannot get along together it should be possible to bring about a dissolution without going to court and proving serious charges against the other person. In many cases these charges are not true, but the accused person does not contest them because he wishes the divorce to be granted. Judges have broad powers of discretion, but the belief in the sanctity of the home and the desire to save it if possible is still a strong consideration. It is a grave question whether or not a home which is kept together contrary to the wishes of the parties is worth saving, as continual discord may be more harmful to the husband and wife, and produce a more serious effect on children, than a divorce.

DEFENSES WHICH ARE A BAR TO DIVORCE

There are several defenses which may be set up to bar divorce. For instance, if a husband, either openly or by passive conduct, encourages his wife to transgress he cannot later set up her infidelity as a cause for divorce, for in legal parlance this is connivance. The parties may not combine to procure a divorce by some false practice, such as one of them doing, or appearing to do, what would otherwise be grounds for divorce. That would be practicing deceit upon the court, and is called collusion. Condonation means to excuse or forgive, and legal condonation is the pardon of an act which would be grounds for divorce while the parties continue to live as if this had not occurred. The offense must cease, however, for the law does not require forgiveness of repeated acts. Recrimination will prevent both parties from obtaining a divorce. For instance, if the husband sets up adultery as an allegation and the wife charges him with cruelty and non-support, and both are proved, neither party can have a divorce, for the court will believe that they are both at fault and will leave them as it finds them. A case in point involved the following facts.[17] A man brought action to obtain a divorce from his wife on the ground that she had deserted him for five years. She proved in defense that before the lapse of five years he married another woman and lived with her. This was sufficient to prove adultery on his part and the divorce was not granted.

RESULTS OF DIVORCE

If a divorce is necessary it is best to consult a good lawyer who will see that the client's rights are protected in every way. The custody of children, property rights, and alimony are all of great moment and should be settled at the time of the divorce. Usually very young children are awarded to the custody of the mother unless she is an improper person to care for them. Later the case may be reopened to further consider this one point if a change in custody is desired. As it then becomes definitely a question of the welfare of the children, the judge should have all the facts available at the time, and often a social worker can be of great assistance in getting this information. Courts do not always make a decree relative to the children and the custody is settled between the parents themselves. This is an unfortunate practice and one that is fraught with future difficulties, particularly if neither parent is able to support the children and they become public charges, for if there is no legal custody the question of settlement is sometimes hard to determine.

[17] Clapp v. Clapp, 97 Mass. 531.

5.

RIGHTS AND OBLIGATIONS AFTER MARRIAGE

WHEN there are no disabilities or statutory prohibitions and a marriage takes place, there are certain rights and obligations which affect both parties. No branch of the law shows greater evidence of the changing times and the effect of modern thought than that which refers to domestic relations. These changes have not come about all at once but have developed through the ages. In the Babylonian civilization women were considered, both physically and mentally, inferior to men, and through the Hebrew, Greek, and Roman progression the same feeling prevailed.

THE RIGHT TO CHASTISE AND RESTRAIN

Blackstone said that in England during his lifetime a man had a right to mildly chastise his wife with a stick no thicker than his thumb, though he added that the exercise of this privilege was mostly limited to the lower classes. Today the husband is looked on as the guardian and protector of his wife and it is unlawful for him to strike her. The husband who does this can be prosecuted for assault and battery, providing his wife will testify in court against him, which she is not always willing to do. Perhaps this reluctance on her part goes back to the time when a husband was lord and master, and carries with it a fear of consequences in the marital relationship, or doubtless some women are definitely masochistic and enjoy being beaten by their husbands. A case in Alabama involved a husband and wife who were emancipated slaves and such treatment was considered a relic of barbarism and not a part of Alabama law.[1] The facts were that the father was chastising his child and his wife interfered as she thought the punishment excessive. The husband struck her twice on the back with a board, and she returned the blow. He was fined for this.

It is said today that a husband can restrain his wife from committing a crime, a tort for which he would be responsible, or perhaps from interfering with the proper training of his children if he is the sole guardian.

A HUSBAND'S RESPONSIBILITY FOR CRIMES

At common law if a woman committed a crime in her husband's presence, or near enough to be under his influence and control, he was responsible and she was excused from blame, as it was presumed that she acted under his direction and was coerced. This rule did not apply to crimes of a grave nature, and today if a woman voluntarily commits a criminal act the responsibility is hers and is not placed upon her husband. But if she is in

[1] Fulgham v. State, 46 Alabama 143.

his presence there may be a presumption of coercion.

Marriage made the husband and wife one at common law, and, as he was the one who represented them both, they were not liable for larceny or burglary from each other, as it was not possible to steal from oneself. Because of their unique relationship, it became the rule that they were not criminally guilty of acts against each other which if perpetrated against anyone else would be crimes. There was an exception to this rule when either one killed the other, for then the killer was liable for homicide.

Today either one is criminally liable for an assault and battery on the other, though the injured party may not recover damages. An Iowa court held that a wife had the right to bring an action against her husband when property was involved but she could not sue him for damages for eleven distinct assaults and batteries.[2]

A husband or wife could not be guilty of arson against the other, for at common law arson meant the burning of the house of another, and they were legally one.[3]

RESPONSIBILITY FOR TORTS

A tort is an unlawful violation of a private legal right not created by contract which gives rise to an action for damages. At common law a husband was liable for torts committed by his wife, even before the marriage, and this liability was ended only by death or divorce. As a general rule wrong acts, as well as crimes, committed in the husband's presence were presumed to have been at

---

[2] Peters v. Peters, 42 Iowa 182.

[3] In September 1935 a judge of a superior court in Maine used this ruling in the case of a man on trial, charged with arson in connection with a fire at his home.

his direction or command. This is changed by statute and in most states a husband is no longer liable for his wife's wrongdoing unless he actually participates, but in a few states he is still liable for slander and assault and battery, even though committed in his absence. Of course, by reason of the unity between the two they were not responsible for torts against each other, but both now have a right of action when there is a wrong committed by a third party against the wife which results in an injury to her. In case of accident she can recover for mental and physical suffering, and the husband can recover for the loss of services and the loss of her society to which he is entitled. At common law a suit for damages for personal injury to her had to be brought jointly, but the husband had to bring suit alone for an injury to himself. In most states a married woman can now bring an action as she could if unmarried.

A HUSBAND'S RIGHT TO THE SOCIETY OF HIS WIFE

A husband has the right of action for damages against anyone who alienates the affections of his wife, or deprives him of her companionship and services by enticing her to leave him or by harboring her. If, however, she is forced through fear of bodily harm to leave him, he cannot recover from anyone who shelters her, and her parents are not liable if they offer their daughter protection in case she is obliged to leave her husband. He can also bring an action for damages known as an action for "criminal conversation" against anyone who has sexual intercourse with his wife, even though there is no loss of service. As a wife is entitled to the society and companionship of her husband, under most modern statutes she can also bring an action for alienation of his affections, but in some states she cannot bring an action against another for enticing him away.

RIGHTS IN PROPERTY

At common law a man upon marriage acquired all the personal property which his wife had in her possession. He was entitled to her earnings, income from stocks, bonds, and bank accounts, if he got them into his possession during his lifetime. At his death they passed to his personal representative, with the exception of her wearing apparel, which she was allowed to keep.

At common law he also acquired an interest in all her real property. He could sell, assign, mortgage, or otherwise dispose of it during marriage without her consent. Real property was liable for his debts, and if he survived her the property became his. If she survived him and he had not disposed of the property during his life, she received it. All estates in which she had a life interest became his, and he could take all rents and profits but he could not dispose of these interests and thereby affect her right to them at his death.

The property and contractual rights of women have changed greatly since the common law was operative, and to understand how much these modifications have meant we should consider the changes under equity, the added powers under legislation called the First Married Women's Act, and the Later Married Women's Act.

TRUST ESTATES FOR WOMEN

Prior to 1800 the Court of Chancery had been interested for centuries in making it possible for a married woman to hold property independently of her husband and to exert over it the same rights which a man or an unmarried woman could exert. This was not so much because the Court of Chancery wished to increase the property rights of married women as it was to give assurance to any person who gave property to a married woman that she could possess it as her own and deal with it independently of her husband, whose common law rights were in conflict with the principles of the Court of Chancery. This court finally achieved its objective and gave to married women practically all the rights which her husband had over property given her for her separate use. This was done by means of an ingenious but simple rule; namely, though a married woman could not hold property in her own right, a trustee could hold it for her benefit. At common law it was still the property of the trustee, but in equity this trustee had to deal with it according to the terms of the trust and in accordance with the wishes of the woman. This became the separate property or separate estate of a married woman. If no trustee was appointed, the husband was at common law the legal owner but he had to hold the property as trustee for his wife. This was a great step toward establishing the legal status of women, and their rights were further extended in this country by statutes.

MARRIED WOMEN'S ACTS

This first legislation gave a woman the right to hold as her separate property any real or personal property which she owned before marriage or acquired by descent, or otherwise, from any person other than her husband. She had sole control of it and could collect rents and receive profits from it. It was not subject to any control of her husband and was exempt from attachment or execution of his debts. The later act, about 1874, though the date varied in the different states, gave a married woman the right to convey property in the same manner and to the same extent that her husband could convey property belonging to him. A rather early case in Maine shows the working of this statute.[4] The husband as plaintiff brought suit for breaking and entering and carrying away several articles of his personal property. It seemed that he had married a woman who owned a farmhouse, articles of furniture, and other personal property, and while they were residing together in this house a third party had entered and removed certain articles. This party introduced evidence to show that the articles belonged to the wife at the time of the marriage and that they had been taken at her direction. The common law giving the husband the title to personal chattels in her possession was not in force, but instead there was a statute which provided that "when any woman possessed of property, real or personal, shall marry, such property shall continue to her and she shall have, hold and possess the same as her separate property." She therefore had entire control over it and the right to dispose of it as she saw fit. Therefore the decision was against the husband as plaintiff.

The decisions in cases which involve a question of the property rights of women vary according to the statutory provision in force in the state at a particular time; that is, whether they have the rights which equity gave, additional privileges under the half-way statutes, or full powers under the later acts.

Although a husband had entire control of his wife's

---

[4] Southard v. Plummer, 36 Maine 64.

personal property at common law, he was responsible for her debts contracted before the marriage as well as those contracted afterward so that the advantage was not all on his side. He was obliged, as he is now, to support his wife and provide her with necessaries suitable to their station in life. Today she is looked upon as his agent and can pledge his credit with tradespeople, contrary to the usual belief, even when he has posted her and stated in the newspaper that he will no longer be responsible for her bills, unless he can prove that the tradespeople saw the notice. *Necessaries* is a relative term depending upon the financial condition of the husband, and the courts have held that expensive clothing bought by the wife of a high-salaried man would be classed as necessaries and in keeping with her station in life, while the same clothing bought by the wife of a laborer would be excessive expense and not necessaries.

DOWER AND CURTESY RIGHTS

In some states today a widow has the same dower rights that she had at common law. That is, she has a one-third interest for life in her husband's real property whether there are children or not. A widow can claim one-half of all the property in some states, and she can waive her dower rights and take her statutory share if she wishes.

At common law a husband on the death of his wife had an estate by curtesy which entitled him to a life estate in all the real property which she held during the marriage, providing the wife had borne a child capable of inheriting. This is changed by statute in most states, but many states still require the signature of both parties to a deed, in order to pass a good title to real estate and to release the respective dower and curtesy rights. A conveyance from husband to wife without a valuable consideration is fraudulent as against his creditors, and sometimes it is considered better policy to make use of the trustee in a transfer of property from husband to wife.

In some states all real or personal property acquired after marriage by either husband or wife is, by statute, community property. This is based on the theory that marriage creates a partnership and all the property which they acquire is for their mutual benefit. The doctrine of community property was not known at common law but originated as a part of the civil or Roman law. It was adopted by Texas and California and a few other western and southwestern states.

HUSBAND AND WIFE AS WITNESSES

At common law, husband and wife were under an absolute disqualification to testify for each other. They could not testify if they were parties to the suit or if the husband or wife of either was a party to the suit, because of the presumption of a personal interest in the result.

The rule today is that parties to a suit may testify in both civil and criminal cases. But statutes in practically all states provide that a husband or wife shall not be compelled, or, without the consent of the other, be allowed to disclose a confidential communication made during the marital relationship, for this is a privileged communication. For instance, if a husband tells his wife that he has robbed a man she cannot be forced to tell this. There is such an identity of interest that the courts do not favor the idea of compelling one party to the marriage to place the partner in jeopardy of punishment for a crime.

RIGHT TO CONTRACT

A husband and wife could not contract with each other at common law as they were legally one person. In fact, a married woman could not contract at all unless her husband had been banished, was a non-resident alien, or was civilly dead, the term used if he had been convicted of a felony. Equity somewhat changed this and gave her certain rights, but even these were limited to contracts relating to her separate estates. That is, she could incur a debt on the credit of separate property which belonged to her at the time the debt was incurred; this property was liable to satisfy the debt. If she borrowed money and had no separate property at the time but in a short time inherited some, in equity, the money which she inherited was not chargeable for the money which she had borrowed.

By later decisions the contracts of a married woman were enforceable against her, otherwise she would have an unfair advantage. A man applied to a bank for a loan of five thousand dollars to be used in his business and offered stock as collateral. The bank declined to make the loan, but told him if his wife wished to borrow the money with the same security she could have the loan. His wife shortly afterward signed a note which authorized him to receive the money and credit it to his business. The bank brought suit against her and the court held that this was an individual contract of the wife as principal and not as surety for him; the fact that she had given him the money did not lessen her liability.[5]

With the consent of her husband a woman could carry on a separate trade or business and could contract with reference to this. Modern statutes have removed the limitations and in most states a woman can now contract with her husband and can bring action against him for failure to perform, as she can against anyone else. While a married woman may become a partner in a firm under modern statutes, all states do not grant her the privilege of becoming a partner with her husband.

WILL MAKING

At common law the will of an unmarried woman was revoked upon marriage. As her personal property became her husband's at that time, she could not devise by will unless her husband was willing for her to dispose of her personal trinkets. According to Blackstone, it was possible for a man to make a will of personal property from very early times but even this was limited and his property was divided into three parts. One part went by law to his lineal descendants, one part to his wife, and he could dispose of the remaining part as he wished. It was not until the statute of wills during the reign of Henry VIII that it was possible to dispose of real estate by will. Now in most states a woman can devise by will as a man can, though in some jurisdictions the property which she has the right to will away is limited, and in a few states the formal consent of the husband is necessary if the will is to be effective. It is important to know the formalities required in each state when making a will; for instance,

[5] Iona Savings Bank v. Boynton, 69 N. H. 77.

the number of witnesses required differs in the various states. Most states by statute require two but some states, especially in New England, require three. Some states also require a seal as well as the signature of the witnesses. Some jurisdictions have held that a will is invalid if one of the witnesses is a beneficiary under the will. Others hold that the will is good and will stand except for the gift to the witness, who will lose the bequest. In a New Hampshire case one of the witnesses to the will was the husband of a beneficiary under the will, and the court held that the legacy rendered him incompetent as a witness and the will invalid.[6] Later cases in New Hampshire have held the will void only as to the particular legacy in the will.

---

[6] Hodgman v. Kittredge, 67 N. H. 264.

6.

RIGHTS AND OBLIGATIONS OF PARENT AND CHILD

NOT only the rights and duties of parents but also the legal responsibilities which the law places on children have changed greatly since ancient times, when a father had the right of life and death over his children. Interest in the welfare of children has increased as civilization has progressed. Though we still have child beatings, crimes against children, and bad adoptions, we also have laws to protect children and legal machinery provided by the State to enforce these laws.

WHEN AN INFANT BECOMES OF AGE

At common law children were legally infants until they became twenty-one years of age. This is still true unless changed by statute, but in many states a girl becomes of age at eighteen though a boy does not reach majority until twenty-one.

The exact moment when an infant becomes of age is

sometimes of considerable importance; for instance, when liquor has been sold, or the right to vote is in question. The rule is that an infant comes of age on the first moment of the day before he celebrates his twenty-first birthday. A court will not consider a fraction of a day in reckoning time, so an infant is regarded as born at the first moment of the day on which he came into the world. In an English case there was a question whether the birthday of a young girl was the fourth or fifth of January, 1805. She was born after the house clock struck twelve, while the parish clock was striking, and before the clock of St. Paul's had begun to strike twelve. It was held that she was born on the fourth because a house clock regulates only domestic affairs, the parish clock was better evidence, but the metropolitan clock was held as implicit evidence of the time.

CUSTODY AND CONTROL

The most fundamental right which parents have is that of custody and control of their minor children. At common law the father had this exclusive right against everyone, including the mother, and he could by will or deed give guardianship of the child to another, as against any right of the mother. This is still the law in some states, but in all but ten the mother and father have equal rights of guardianship and on the death of the father the mother has exclusive control. A New Hampshire court held that this joint guardianship continues even after separation.[1] In this instance the parents were divorced but no order was made relating to the custody of the child. The mother lived in New Hampshire and the father

[1] White v. White, 77 N. H. 26.

placed the child outside of the state. The decision was that the joint guardianship conferred by statute in 1911 was not dependent upon the continuance of the marital relationship and could only be terminated during the minority of the child by the death of one parent or by a decree of the court. Therefore, while the mother was domiciled in New Hampshire and possessed equal rights of custody with the father, the child's domicile in this state was not lost by the removal of the child to the domicile of the father in another state.

The Court of Chancery in England considered the welfare of the child and took the custody from a father who was found to be unfit. Unless the child was heir to property, however, the Court of Chancery did not usually intercede; so the fate of the children of the masses still remained in the common law courts.

THE FATHER'S DUTY TO SUPPORT

At common law there was no obligation resting upon a father to support his children to the extent that legal action could be taken to force him to discharge this duty. It was held to be only a moral obligation and even the statute passed during the reign of Queen Elizabeth was restrictive as it provided that no one was under a duty to support his child, except as to necessaries, unless the child was unable to work through infancy, disease, or accident. This duty is now regulated by statute, and usually upon the death of the father it falls upon the mother if she is in suitable circumstances. At common law a third person who had furnished a child with necessaries could not recover from the father unless he could show that the father had given the child the right to pledge his credit. In an old English case the facts were that a father sent his minor son to London with the expectation that he would enroll on a ship.[2] He gave him money and instructed him to stay at a certain hotel while waiting for the ship, but the son went to another hotel which he thought was more economical and nearer the docks. He stayed there for fifteen weeks, and then the innkeeper brought suit against his father for his board. The opinion of the court was that a father who gives no authority and enters into no contract is not liable for goods supplied to his son. There might seem to be a moral obligation but there could be no such inference from a legal standpoint.

If parents were living apart because of the father's misconduct, he was chargeable only for the necessaries of the child living with the mother, on the theory that he was responsible for her necessaries and while the child was living with her he would be responsible for the necessaries of the child also. Our courts are more liberal and hold the father responsible to a third party when the child is away from him. Some jurisdictions have gone so far as to hold the father liable for support after divorce even when no express provision has been made for this. A man deserted his wife and three-months-old child and contributed nothing toward the support of either.[3] The mother went to live in Colorado, while the father lived in Minnesota. She obtained a divorce in Minnesota and the custody of the child was awarded to her. No provision was made for the maintenance of the child, who became ill with tuberculosis and needed special care. The question involved was, would the law imply a promise

---

[2] Shelton v. Springett, Court of Common Pleas, 11 C. B. 452. (English case).

[3] Spencer v. Spencer, Minn. 105 N. W. 483.

on the father's part to pay for the child's care? There is some conflict on this point and the decisions in some states do not so hold, but by the weight of authority the father's liability is not impaired by the decree of divorce giving custody to the mother.[4] If he refuses to pay, she can recover, for the law implies a promise to pay because of the benefit conferred upon the child.

In the absence of statute there is no obligation on a child to support his parents.

THE RIGHT TO EARNINGS

Along with the parents' right of custody is the right to the services and earnings of a minor child. We find that foreign people and others of poor economic status often avail themselves of this right and insist that a child shall become a breadwinner and help with the burden of the family as soon as he is old enough for this. Probably many children have been started on the way to delinquency by demanding parents who have failed to recognize the child's right to have a small amount of spending money from his own earnings.

A New Jersey court upheld a mother's right to the earnings of her child when the father was dead.[5] Action was brought by the mother to recover compensation for the work and labor of her son, a minor, who had worked for one Allen at his request. Allen contended that action could not be brought by the mother even though the minor lived at home and was cared for by his mother. The opinion of the court was that the mother succeeded

---

[4] Massachusetts, Rhode Island, Indiana, Kansas, and Iowa have held there was no liability.

[5] Osborne v. Allen, 26 N. J. 388.

the father in the duty of caring for her son and she also succeeded to the father's right to his earnings. It is interesting to note that at common law the decision would have been contrary to this. Blackstone disposed of a mother's rights in such a situation by saying that as a mother she was entitled to no power but only reverence and respect.

EMANCIPATION

If a child has become emancipated, the parents can not recover his wages. Emancipation can be brought about in three ways: if a father agrees that the child shall be free from his control, or abandons or fails to support the child, or the child consummates a valid marriage, he is legally emancipated.

The question of the validity of a marriage came up in a suit which was brought for unlawfully enticing away the plaintiff's daughter and depriving the plaintiff of her services from March 29, 1879, to September 2, 1882, when she became twenty-one. It was proved that the daughter had been lawfully married on March 29, 1879.[6] The court said that the marriage of an infant if above the legal age of consent, as she was, is valid though it was contracted in defiance of parental wishes and authority. Therefore, a new relationship was created by the marriage and the father was no longer entitled to the earnings of his daughter as she was emancipated. There have been other decisions holding an opposite view,[7] but most decisions are in accord with the New Hampshire case.

---

[6] Aldrich v. Bennett, 63 N. H. 415.
[7] White v. Henry, 24 Maine 531.

RIGHT TO RECOVER FOR INJURY

It follows that if the father has the right to the earnings of the child he has a valuable property interest in the child, and on this interest he can recover for services and earnings if the child is injured or killed. There are really two causes of action arising: one to the father, to recover damages for loss of services during the period of illness or sometimes, in case of the child's death, until the child would have reached majority; the other to the child, giving him the right to recover for injury, pain, and personal loss. If a child is too young to work and there is therefore no loss in services but the injury causes expense for nursing and medical care, the general rule is that the parent can recover for this. If a female child is seduced the father can recover damages for the shame and embarrassment caused him, as well as for the loss of services, and he has the right of action against anyone who entices his child away.

NONLIABILITY FOR TORTIOUS ACTS

A parent is not liable for the wrongful or tortious acts of his child even though they involve injury and financial damage to property. Consequently, if a child breaks the windows of a neighbor's house by throwing stones, or otherwise destroys property, there is no legal liability though the father may feel that he has a moral obligation to pay for the damages. Neither is a father liable if his child takes his automobile without his knowledge, and while driving it runs into another car. A very old case attempted to hold the father liable for the wrongful act of his child on the theory that the child was like a vicious animal and since the father knew this, he would be liable, just as he would be for the damage caused by a vicious dog. However, this reasoning did not prevail. The father is responsible if a wrongful act is done at his order, for then the child is his agent and they can be sued jointly; but in general the child is responsible for his own acts and can be sued in the name of his guardian or next friend.

THE DOCTRINE OF ATTRACTIVE NUISANCES

The rule known as the Doctrine of Attractive Nuisances gives recognition to the fact that certain mechanical devices have an attraction for children. This originated in an old English case in which the facts were that the owner of a wagon left it standing by the curb and a small boy got in the wagon and was injured when the horse ran away. The boy was guilty of wrongful conduct in trespassing on another's property, but the court held that the cart invited the small boy and the owner was liable for the boy's injury. Since that time the Doctrine of Attractive Nuisances has been followed in most jurisdictions, first in railroad turntable cases, and more recently in cases involving automobiles which have been left unoccupied with the engine running. The courts are not in entire agreement on the turntable cases, for a New Hampshire court held that the railroad was under no duty to keep the premises safe for a mere trespasser, and that the trespasser's being a child made no difference.[8] This is quite opposed to the ruling of a Minnesota court which held that the child did not occupy the position of

[8] Frost v. Railroad, 64 N. H. 220.

an ordinary trespasser—the defendant knew that a turntable is very attractive to children and when in motion very dangerous and by leaving it unfastened and unguarded was holding it out as an allurement.[9] The child could not be blamed for yielding to the temptation, so the railroad was liable for not giving protection to the child.

THE DOG—YESTERDAY AND TODAY

The small boy's friend, the dog, has come in for legal recognition also. Formerly when a dog bit a man he was tried and executed, that is, if he was a vicious dog and habitually bit people. He would not be disposed of on the first offense, however, on the theory that "every dog is entitled to one bite." Today the dog is not tried but the owner may be sued for damages and even then it is necessary to show that the owner knew that the dog was vicious.

CRIMINAL INTENT NECESSARY

It is necessary to have a criminal intent in order to commit a crime. At common law a child under seven was presumed to be unable to commit a crime, but between the ages of seven and fourteen it was possible to show that he did intend the consequences of his act, and if over the age of fourteen he was presumed to have sufficient capacity to commit a crime; he then had to show nonexistence of criminal intent for the wrongful act in order to escape liability. Children as young as ten and

[9] Keefe v. Railroad, 21 Minn. 207.

twelve have been hanged for their wrongful acts, both in England and in this country.

PROPERTY RIGHTS OF INFANTS

With the father's duty to support goes the corresponding right of the child to receive care and to inherit from the father. At common law inheritance rights were affected by the feudal system, and at first only the eldest son had the right of inheritance. Later all the sons were capable of inheriting, but none of the daughters were. In this country, unless there is a will, lineal descendants inherit equally. At common law an unborn child had no right to acquire and hold property, and so could not inherit if born after the death of the father. This has been changed by statute in this country, and a posthumous child will inherit equally with those born during the life of the father.

LIABILITIES OF INFANTS

In order to protect infants while they are inexperienced and immature from the acts of persons who may be designing, the law has placed certain privileges at their disposal. The most important of these is the power to avoid contracts. The general rule is that an infant is not bound by his contracts, and some states hold that however great the benefit received, his infancy is a complete defense. One state at least has held that the infant who has received benefits is liable for their fair value.[10] This is based, not upon the contract, but on an implied

[10] Hall v. Butterfield, 59 N. H. 354.

promise to pay for benefits received. While it seems only right that very young children should be protected and be given the power to avoid the results of ill-considered acts, a different situation arises when a person from sixteen to twenty-one is involved. Then the infancy may be used as a means of defrauding innocent tradesmen who have been deceived as to the true age of the child. An infant is liable if he misstates his age and says that he is older than he is. However, the action then is not based on a contract, but recovery is possible because of deceit. An infant can repudiate a contract any time before he receives a benefit. For example, if he contracts to buy a set of books he can disaffirm any time before receiving the books. The liability of an infant for necessities furnished him again brings up the question of what are necessaries besides food, clothing, and shelter. One court held that when an infant gave a party to his friends at college this was an indulgence and not a necessity. Taken as a whole the laws relating to infants present a good deal of inconsistency, for even in the same jurisdiction the decisions have not been uniform.

THE ILLEGITIMATE CHILD

In considering the responsibility of parents to their children we have to consider the illegitimate child also. Some of the earlier civilizations recognized the right of the illegitimate child to inherit property under certain conditions, and what is still more important, to receive recognition from the father. The ecclesiastics tried to introduce into the common law courts the rule that these children became legitimate upon the subsequent marriage of their parents. This was very distasteful to the barons because it interfered with the rights of inheritance, but it is the rule in most states now and many children have been thus legitimatized. At common law the illegitimate child was looked upon as nobody's child, but had the domicile of the mother. The mother also had custody and was entitled to the child's wages, but until the time of Queen Elizabeth she was not obliged to give support. Of course the father had no obligation to support, because legally he was not the father. This child of nobody could inherit neither from his father nor his mother, nor could the parents inherit from him, as he had no heirs except from his own body. By statute in most states he can now inherit from his mother, and in some states where the legislation is particularly advanced he can inherit from his father, though paternity must be established by court procedure. If a woman is married there is a strong presumption that any child born to her is legitimate, but this may be overcome by convincing proof that her husband is not the father; for example, if he is impotent or has been away from his wife for such a time that it is impossible for him to be the father. Today most states have statutes which place the responsibility of support on the father, but all too often no action is taken to establish paternity, which has to be determined before liability can be fixed. In some states the policy of accepting a lump sum settlement rather than a weekly or monthly payment prevails, but since these lump sum payments are generally small the burden falls in time on the mother or on some agency. Altogether, the illegitimate child has more consideration than in the past. Many states make provision for investigating and licensing foster homes that board illegitimate children; better physical care is provided by social agencies than formerly, and each mother's problem is considered on an individual case-work basis. Many of these children are adopted and bring a great deal of happiness to their adoptive parents as well as gaining for themselves a sense of security and a legal status.

7.

THE STATE AND THE CHILD

THE State has a sovereign power, by means of its legislative acts and the authority vested in its governmental divisions, to protect the child whose parents, because of their mistakes and failures, neglect to do so. The State also assumes certain responsibilities for all children.

LAWS TO SAFEGUARD HEALTH

A child is not aware that the moment he comes into the world the laws which control his whole life are in operation. For instance, the law provides that a physician or other qualified person, licensed under the statutes of the State, must officiate at his birth; the birth must be recorded, that the child may be on record as a legal personality. Pure food laws and properly tested milk give him adequate protection from infection, and health laws make vaccination necessary before he may enter school. Here again, through periodic examinations and health instruction given by doctors, dentists, and nurses, the child continues on the road toward health. Mental as well as physical health is considered, and in many states the Department of Education provides clinics where mental abilities can be ascertained and emotional problems adjusted.

SCHOOL LAWS

The statutes prescribe the age at which a child shall enter school and how long he must continue there before he can go to work. In many states it is compulsory to attend grade school until sixteen, but there are exceptions to this rule. In most states a child can leave at fourteen if he has finished a specific grade, if it is necessary for him to work in order to help maintain the family, or if he is physically or mentally handicapped so that he is incapable of learning.

LAWS TO REGULATE EMPLOYMENT

The laws regulating employment have gone hand in hand with those prescribing compulsory education, and there is a long history back of this which is pretty dark in spots. The Puritans and the Quakers felt that idleness was a sin, and this attitude led to an exploitation of children in industry during the early years of this country's development. New England led with a record of children ten years of age and even younger working in the cotton mills for fourteen hours at a time. This was to teach them a useful trade and make them capable of supporting themselves.

In 1836 Massachusetts passed a law making compulsory school attendance necessary for at least three months of the year. Other states followed with provisions regulating the age of employment, but it was not until about fifty years ago that birth certificates were required as proof of age. There were many parents who falsified the age of their children, and altogether state legislation failed to cure the evils of child labor.

The first federal child labor law was enacted in 1916 and set the minimum age for employment at fourteen. This law was based on the power of Congress to regulate interstate commerce and was declared unconstitutional by the United States Supreme Court in 1918 in the well-known Hammer v. Dagenhart decision. The Supreme Court declared: "Commerce consists of intercourse and traffic and includes the transportation of persons and property, as well as the purchase, sale, and exchange of commodities. The making of goods and the mining of coal are not commerce, nor does the fact that these things are to be afterwards shipped or used in interstate commerce make their production a part thereof. Over interstate transportation or its incidents, the regulatory power of Congress is ample but the production of articles intended for interstate commerce is a matter of local regulation." [1] This placed the responsibility back on the states, a practice which is so widely advocated today along other lines.

The second federal child labor law was passed in 1919. This was based on the taxing power of Congress and levied a tax of 10 per cent on the profits if children were employed in violation of the age-and-hour standards of the bill. It likewise was held unconstitutional in 1922 and the Supreme Court again declared that under the Constitution this was a matter to be regulated by the states.[2]

---

[1] This decision was recently reversed (1941).
[2] Bailey v. Drexel Furniture Co.

Since that time there have been other attempts to control child labor. In 1924 there was a proposed amendment to the Constitution which, as with all amendments, required a ratification by three-fourths of the states in order to become a law. As this was ratified by only twenty-eight states,[8] it never went into effect. In 1933 under the National Recovery Act an attempt was made to meet the unemployment situation by prohibiting, with a few exceptions, the employment of children under sixteen. This was declared unconstitutional in Schechter Poultry Corporation v. United States.

In 1938 further federal legislation was introduced and Congress passed the Fair Labor Standards Act or the Wages and Hours Act, which became operative in October 1938. This prohibits the shipment in interstate commerce of goods made in establishments that have employed child labor within thirty days prior to shipment. Oppressive child labor means the employment of children under sixteen by anyone other than their parents, or the employment of children under eighteen in occupations which the Chief of the Children's Bureau shall declare hazardous or detrimental to their health or well-being. Children employed in agriculture or as actors in motion pictures or theatrical productions are not affected, and a large group of children who are employed

[8]

Arizona	1925	Kentucky	1937	Ohio	1933
Arkansas	1924	Maine	1933	Oklahoma	1933
California	1925	Michigan	1933	Oregon	1933
Colorado	1931	Minnesota	1933	Pennsylvania	1933
Idaho	1935	Montana	1927	Utah	1935
Illinois	1933	Nevada	1937	Washington	1933
Indiana	1935	New Hampshire	1933	West Virginia	1933
Iowa	1933	New Jersey	1933	Wisconsin	1925
Kansas	1937	New Mexico	1937	Wyoming	1935
		North Dakota	1933		

in intrastate industry and mercantile establishments, as well as many others, are not included.

It is almost impossible to obtain accurate figures on child labor, but the 1930 census showed that there were more than 600,000 children from ten to fifteen years of age that were gainfully employed.[4] This was considered an underestimate of the total number because the census did not include children under ten. Seventy per cent of these children were employed in agriculture or as unpaid family workers. Many of these will still remain unaffected by the Federal Wages and Hours Act, but child labor in industrial plants which ship goods in interstate commerce will be ended. This act brings about a coöperative plan of control which was not possible under the separate state laws; it is administered by the Federal Childrens' Bureau in coöperation with state and local offices, provides for investigation and inspection of employment, and penalizes any employer who violates the provisions of the act.

A SPECIAL COURT FOR CHILDREN

Laws for the protection of animals antedated laws to protect children, and in 1875 when a little girl was cruelly beaten in New York she had to be considered as a little animal in order to receive legal protection. This resulted in the establishment of agencies all over the country for the prevention of cruelty to children. In time the essential rights and protection of children became so important that a special court, called the juvenile court, was established. The first one was in Cook County, Illinois, in 1899, and this was quickly followed by similar

[4] The figures based on the 1940 census are not yet available.

courts in New York, Indiana, New Jersey, and other states, until at the present time all states make provision for hearings on juvenile cases. The juvenile court was started as an experiment in legal procedure and has continued on that basis. For its precedent it had the court of equity and, like it, was founded on the desire to break away from a harsh and rigid procedure, which in this instance was the application of criminal justice to children. This court was therefore based on the concept of equity, that is, a consideration of the welfare of the child instead of punishment for the offense; it looked upon the offender as an individual and his acts as symptoms which needed to be understood. In other words, the legal system which prescribed rigid punishment acted in a new light if the offender was a child. We should not lose sight of the fact, however, that though this court takes a social viewpoint in the exercise of its duty, it is nevertheless a court and its function is primarily a judicial one. It has the power to exercise this function only within the limitation and jurisdiction prescribed by the statute, notwithstanding the fact that its procedure may be less formal and its rules of evidence less rigid than other courts.

The jurisdiction of the juvenile court includes neglected, dependent, and delinquent children. The 1929 White House Conference Committee on Juvenile Delinquency defined the acts which came under the early jurisdiction as: "Any such juvenile misconduct that might be dealt with under the law." A delinquent child is often defined as: "Any child who violates any law of the State or who is incorrigible, knowingly associates with vicious and immoral persons, or is growing up in idleness and crime." A dependent child is one who is without support or who begs or receives alms. The term "neglect" is broad and includes physical, moral, and usually medical neglect. The juvenile court may be a separate court, or a division or session of another court, and sometimes in serving rural areas it is on a county basis.

JURISDICTION OF THE JUVENILE COURT

The jurisdiction of some juvenile courts has been extended to include cases of adoptions, of mental defectives, and of illegitimate children. There is some variation in the age when jurisdiction can be acquired, though in about half the states these courts can take jurisdiction of a child at any time before the eighteenth birthday, and when custody is once given by order of the court it generally continues through minority. It is a well-accepted concept that the juvenile court jurisdiction should be exclusive up to the age of eighteen, but in many states children who have committed a serious offense are bound over to the higher court and the old criminal procedure is applied. Hearings are then no longer private, and instead of considering the child according to juvenile court standards he is looked upon as a criminal.

OBJECTIVES

The person who is sitting in this court, whether judge or referee, should be especially qualified for the work. He should have not only legal training but also a social consciousness and a knowledge of the aids which science has developed toward an understanding of children. Therefore, the investigation of a social worker should be a requirement, for this will bring the court a knowledge of the family background, environmental factors, school history, and the child's relationship to his family and the community. There should be a medical examination, and, finally, the searching inquiry of a qualified psychologist and psychiatrist for a better understanding of the child and the problem. When this is required, the judge will be in possession of all the facts that intelligence and science can bring to the problem and is less apt to make an unwise decision; for instance, a child of very low intelligence will probably not be sent to a correctional institution when training in a school for the feebleminded will provide more adequate care.

PENDING DISPOSITION

In many states the law provides that a child cannot be held in jail pending the hearing. In large cities children are held in detention homes or in private foster homes when it is necessary to take them into custody at once; for example, if they are runaways and their appearance in court cannot be relied upon, or their delinquency is very serious and their release will endanger the public, or they must be held as important witnesses.

PROBATION OFFICERS

With the properly equipped juvenile court the law provides for one or more persons to act as probation officers. These officers sometimes assist in the investigation, and, if a child remains in his own home, act as friends to counsel and advise both the child and his parents. This can be effective or not, according to the personality of the probation officer, who is a very important part of the court system.

There have been a good many cases attacking the constitutionality of the juvenile court law, either on the ground that the parent's legal rights as custodian are violated, unless he is made a party to the proceedings, or that the right of a jury trial is denied. A case in Illinois a few years after the passage of the act shows the early attitude toward this particular legislation. In this instance a writ of *habeas corpus* was brought by one Joseph Schwartz against the superintendent of the St. Charles Home for Boys for unlawfully restraining his son, Samuel Schwartz, fourteen years of age. It was shown that the father lived in Chicago with his family, consisting of his wife and two children, that he provided a good home for them, and that he supplied them with the necessities of life. The son, Samuel, was charged with repeated indecent assaults upon two girls in violation of the criminal code of the state, and he was committed to the St. Charles Home for Boys until twenty-one years of age. The parents were ordered to bring the boy to court but they were not made parties to the proceeding or charged with the omission of any parental duty. The court agreed that the commitment was according to the provision of the act to regulate the treatment and control of dependent, neglected, and delinquent children in force July 1, 1899, for Samuel was a delinquent boy within the meaning of the act, but that it was not within the power of the state to seize any child under the age of sixteen who had committed a misdemeanor punishable under the criminal code of the state by fine, and take him from his home and the custody of his father as it was an infringement upon parental rights. Though the court admitted that an extraordinary exigency could justify the state in supplanting the father as the natural custodian and protector of his son, it did not exist in this case. Further opinion stated by the court was to the effect that it did not hold the statute regulating the disposition to be made of delinquent children to be unconstitutional *in toto* as to every parent and to all children but in this case the constitutional rights of the father had been infringed and the detention of Samuel could not be upheld.[5] The law was amended in 1907, and later cases in Illinois sustained the constitutionality of the Juvenile Court Act. Between 1899 and 1909 the validity of such laws was passed upon in Florida, Idaho, Pennsylvania, and Utah, and was sustained by the Supreme Courts in those states.

MOTHERS' AID LEGISLATION

Great social progress, backed by legal provision, has brought about protection for another group of children. When dependent children first became a matter of public concern they were apprenticed, and a little later cared for in orphanages. More recently the plan of placement in foster homes has developed and along with it the system of mothers' aid or mothers' pension, which gives aid to mothers so that children can be cared for in their own homes. This took the place of some form of poor relief, and is included in the security legislation under the provision of aid to dependent children, which will be taken up in more detail later. The constitutionality of this legislation has been attacked on the ground that

[5] People ex rel—Schwartz v. McLain (Supreme Court of Illinois 1905).

these laws make an arbitrary selection of beneficiaries or that public funds are not applied for a public use.

One of the early decisions on the first point was in Washington in 1916. Rose Snyder had received an allowance under the Mothers' Pension Act in October of 1913 because she had been deserted by her husband. A later act in 1915 provided for allowances to indigent mothers whose husbands were dead or incarcerated in a penal institution or insane hospital, or whose husbands were unable because of total disability to support them. Mothers who had been deserted were not included. The court held that the first law did not provide for all classes of indigent mothers and that the second one was not unconstitutional as class legislation on the grounds of arbitrary selection. It further held that the state had a right to provide for the care of its indigent in any way it wished and at the discretion of the legislature.[6] The responsibility of the county commissioners was decided in a case in Utah in 1922.[7] There was a law authorizing the county commissioners to provide funds annually for the support of widowed mothers. It was held that this law was mandatory and put a duty upon them which was not fulfilled when they provided for widowed mothers out of a fund to provide for indigent and dependent poor, including widowed mothers.

The question of divorce and custody also was involved in one mothers' aid case. This concerned the children of Charles and Gunde Koopman, who were divorced. The father had deserted his family and was a fugitive from justice, and the mother had been given

---

[6] Snyder Petition, 93 Wash. 59.

[7] Startup & Harmon et al—Commissioners of Utah County—203 Pac. 637.

the custody of the children at the time of the divorce. The mother had a right to relief unless barred by divorce. The Supreme Court decided that the purpose of the statute was to provide for the welfare of dependent children whose parents could not care for them and the Mothers' Pension Act was held to apply to a mother with dependent children although she had been divorced.[8]

OTHER GROUPS OF HANDICAPPED CHILDREN

The state gives protection to other groups of handicapped children in a different way. There are more than ten million physically and mentally handicapped children in the United States. The individual states have a responsibility toward them to see that their latent abilities are developed and that they become assets to the community and state instead of liabilities. This group includes those who are deaf or hard of hearing, blind or have partial sight, crippled children, or those suffering from tuberculosis or serious cardiac disturbances, as well as the group included under the generic term of mentally deficient. This last group is composed of those who are feebleminded, such as the idiots and imbeciles who can never be socially or economically adequate, many morons and borderline individuals who are also inadequate, and many other morons who with training and supervision may become efficient enough to manage their affairs and meet the stress and strain of life. All these groups present problems of adjustment, and in working

[8] In Re Koopman—146 Minn. 36—177 N. W. 777. Reference was made to an earlier decision in a Minnesota case (Spencer v. Spencer) in which the mother's rights were not impaired by divorce and custody.

with the many complications involved the social worker is prone to forget that legal provision accompanies social planning and is an important part of any program.

LEGAL PROVISION

Legislative acts have established various state departments and have made provisions for the care of the blind, deaf and dumb, crippled, and the feebleminded, either in institutions or foster homes, according to the needs of the child. The care and education should be broad if the physical and mental powers are to be developed to their fullest capacity, and this involves a knowledge of the needs. It is possible to obtain this knowledge through studies authorized by the legislature and undertaken by various departments of health, education, and welfare, working toward a coördinated legislative program. Three processes are involved: first, the handicapped child must be discovered and reported to a central agency; secondly, he must have medical care and necessary appliances; and, lastly, he must have education, which includes guidance to assure proper selection and training, and placement with supervision. This is the ideal program and is not provided for every handicapped child, but the goal seems nearer since the Federal Government has become interested in the welfare of its children and through the Social Security Act is assuming some of the burdens formerly carried by the states.

LEGISLATION RELATING TO THE FEEBLEMINDED AND THE INSANE

There has been a good deal of legislation pertaining to the care, education, commitment, and even sterilization of the feebleminded, but the early laws made no distinction between the insane and the feebleminded. As a class they were all considered persons *non compos mentis* and included under the term insane, which was the legal term covering mental unsoundness of any sort. When insanity was set up as a defense in a criminal case the legal test, according to a rule laid down in McNaughten's case in England nearly one hundred years ago, was the so-called test of right and wrong. That rule is: "If an offender has sufficient mental capacity to know that the act which he is about to commit is wrong and deserves punishment, and to apply that knowledge at the time when the act is committed, he is not in the eyes of the criminal law insane but is responsible." This test is followed in many jurisdictions today.

It seems quite clear that legal concepts have not kept pace with knowledge in the fields of medicine and of psychiatry. Even lay persons today realize that there is a vast difference between the insane and the feebleminded and that it is sometimes as necessary to provide protection from those individuals as to provide care for them. This is especially true of the defective delinquent, who is often implicated in sex crimes of the most revolting sort. The decision, which involves punishment or care, should not be based on a fine legal point but should be determined from consideration of the mental and emotional adjustment of the individual. Every state should have a law similar to the one in Massachusetts which provides that any person who is to be tried for a felony must have an examination by a psychiatrist. After the examination the court should be guided by this opinion in determining the release or restraint of the individual. If this takes power from the court, it also divides the responsibility and would assure a smaller number of dangerous persons at large.

EDUCATION AND TRAINING OF THE FEEBLEMINDED

In Institutions.— During childhood the education of the feebleminded can often be more satisfactorily supplied in an institution where the child has to compete only with those of like intelligence and can be taught to do many tasks which give him happiness and at the same time make some contribution to society. These institutions are a responsibility of the State and generally either accept children directly on application from parents, public officials, or other sources; or require or permit commitment in the same manner as for the insane; others provide for commitment through some judicial tribunal, which necessitates a petition setting forth the facts. This is followed by a hearing with the testimony of either physicians or psychologists, who can give the court the benefit of their knowledge as specialists.

In the Community.— The time has passed when specialists feel that every mentally defective child should be in an institution. With the exception of the helpless, low-grade cases, many such children can be trained to compete with their fellow men and pursue their affairs in the world with ordinary prudence.[9]

The Department of Education in many states has assumed a responsibility towards these children and

---

[9] The British Royal Commission on the feebleminded defined a feebleminded person as anyone who may be capable of earning a living under favorable circumstances, but is incapable, from mental defect existing from birth or from an early age, of competing on equal terms with normal fellows; or of managing himself and his affairs with ordinary prudence.

provides special classes and education in hand and manual training rather than in academic work. Registration with this board is important and is required in some states so there can be information concerning the number of children and the place of residence.

STERILIZATION OF THE FEEBLEMINDED

Marriage of the feebleminded is prohibited in some states, and sterilization, which is a much more effective method of preventing parenthood, is permitted in thirty-one. The first eugenic sterilization bill was introduced in Michigan in 1897. Pennsylvania passed a law which was vetoed, and Indiana adopted a law in 1907 which was later declared unconstitutional; so Washington and California, both in 1909, were the first states which passed effective laws, and California probably has a record of more such operations than any other state in the country. The United States Supreme Court sustained the legality of eugenic sterilization in a case which came up on appeal from Virginia. Carrie Buck, an eighteen-year-old feebleminded girl, the child of a feebleminded woman and the mother of a feebleminded child, was in an institution and sterilized against her will. Justice Holmes in handing down the decision said, "It is better for all the world if instead of waiting to execute degenerate offspring for crime or to let them starve for their imbecility, society can prevent those who are manifestly unfit from continuing their kind. Three generations of imbeciles are enough."

There is a great deal of misinformation about this particular subject, both as to the social implications and the legal safeguards. In the states which permit sterilization there is often a fear that anyone who goes to a state institution will undergo this operation, but as a matter of fact many defectives in state institutions are not proper subjects for sterilization. Helpless epileptics and idiots, though included under the terms of the law, as a practical matter need custodial care for life and therefore should not be considered for sterilization. One state which has a very comprehensive state law limits the operation to anyone who by the laws of heredity is "the probable potential parent of socially inadequate offspring likewise affected." It further safeguards the individual by providing for the consent of the guardian and for a hearing which shall be a matter of record, with the right of appeal and preservation of all constitutional rights. The hearing must be conducted before a board and detailed proof of heredity is necessary. If this cannot be produced because relatives are dead or are foreign born and inaccessible, the operation is not possible.[10]

LEGAL AND SOCIAL RESPONSIBILITY OF THE STATE

In any consideration of the responsibility of the State toward its children it should be quite clear that the relationship combines the social and legal aspects, and at times there is such a coalescence of the two that they seem synonymous inasmuch as both fields of endeavor involve the rules of living as they apply to the individual.

[10] The New Hampshire law contains these provisions.

8.

GUARDIANSHIP

THOUGH the State may be looked upon as the ultimate parent, it is sometimes necessary, because of various circumstances, for a court to appoint an individual to assume control of a child or of another individual. *Guardianship* is the legal term given to the relationship whereby one person is entrusted by law with the care of the person or property, or the person and property of another. It implies protective authority over one who, due to his age or some other cause, is unable to look after himself. The person under guardianship may be a minor, a spendthrift, or a person *non compos mentis*.

GUARDIANSHIP UNDER THE FEUDAL SYSTEM

In some form or other guardianship has existed from very early times. Under the feudal system in England the baronial lords imposed certain restrictions on the vassals who were required to give military service, thereby obtaining revenue, by means of an arrangement called *guardianship in chivalry*. If a male heir was under twenty-one or a female heir was under sixteen at the death of the father, the lord was entitled to take the property into his possession and appropriate all the profits of it during the minority of the ward, on the ground that it was a reasonable compensation for the services which the minor, because of his age, could not render. The lord also had the right to bring about a suitable marriage and appropriate whatever he could for this service. If the ward refused to pay him for this service, he could recover from the ward's property; if the ward married without the lord's consent, he could demand a still larger forfeiture than if he brought about the marriage. This form of guardianship applied to military tenure only and was abolished by statute in 1660. *Guardianship in socage* was another vagary of the feudal system and arose when an infant acquired lands by descent which were held in socage; that is, the tenants of the land were obliged to give a certain portion of the crops or to plow the lord's land.[1] If the infant was under fourteen when he became heir to the land it was given to his next of kin who could not possibly inherit from him, and this relative had authority over the person of the heir, his land, and such property as crops and timber which had been cut. When the infant became fourteen he could choose his guardian.

TESTAMENTARY GUARDIANSHIP

After guardianship in chivalry was abolished a father, who was the natural guardian, was permitted, either by deed or will, to name a guardian for his child, and this guardian acted during the child's minority. This emphasis upon the power of a father shows that at common law a mother did not have equal rights with a father in the

---

[1] Guardianship by chivalry never existed in this country but guardianship in socage was recognized in early days in New York State, though it was not common in any of the other states.

guardianship of their child. A person appointed in this way by the father was called a testamentary guardian. Testamentary guardians can be appointed today and some states require no judicial confirmation, while in others if a testamentary guardian has been nominated the person has to qualify; that is, the appointment is subject to the probate of the will and to the approval of the court; in addition, the remaining parent must have notice before the appointment is made.

STATUTORY GUARDIANSHIP

In England the court of chancery had jurisdiction over the person and property of infants; in this country the courts of equity took over this function quite early; today special courts such as probate, surrogate, or orphans' courts have jurisdiction and the judges of these courts have the power to appoint a guardian over the person and the estate of infants. These guardians are given the legal term of *statute guardians* because their powers and duties are controlled by state statutes. These correspond to the chancery guardians of England.

GUARDIAN AD LITEM

Sometimes a person assumes the right to act as guardian without any legal authority, and if there is property or if civil rights are violated he is held to account just the same as a legal guardian would be. If there is no legal guardian or anyone acting in that capacity the court can appoint a *guardian ad litem* to prosecute or defend for an infant in any suit in which he is involved, for if he has no guardian there would be no one to defend his rights as he cannot appear in person. The duties extend only to the particular suit in question. A *guardian ad litem* is often appointed in adoption cases. If neither parent is living and there is no guardian or near kin to give consent, the court can appoint a suitable person to act as guardian ad litem and consent to the adoption. This guardian has no authority beyond the adoption proceedings.

GUARDIANSHIP A TRUST RELATIONSHIP

As we know that the chancery court, which was based on justice and equitable treatment, had the power to appoint a guardian, we can conclude that the best interest of the child was of paramount consideration. Though the father's wishes were usually respected, the court had plenty of authority to appoint a suitable person even against the wishes of the father. The status of a guardian is one of personal trust and the relationship is similar to that of trustee as well as of parent, though the guardian has no right to his ward's services or earnings. Guardianship cannot be assigned though the relationship may be terminated by the resignation of the guardian. The statutes of many states allow institutional guardianship, by a home or organization incorporated under the laws of the state, but judges in some of these states appoint an individual only, believing that the relationship should be a personal one and not merely a perfunctory arrangement.[2]

---

[2] The probate courts in New Hampshire follow this rule and do not appoint an institution as guardian.

INFANTS' RIGHT TO CHOOSE

As previously stated, at common law if the infant was over fourteen he had the right to choose the person whom he would like as guardian. This is usually true today, and unless a person is unsuitable the judge does not have arbitrary powers. In a Connecticut case a minor over fourteen petitioned for a guardian who was not approved by the judge, and she was told to choose another.[8] She refused to do this and the judge appointed someone. She brought suit to remove the person, and on appeal the Supreme Court held that the judge did not have the power to appoint a guardian on her refusal to choose a second person when the first one was suitable. The welfare of the minor is paramount, and if a guardian is unsuitable a judge has sufficient authority to protect the child.

JURISDICTION RESTRICTED BY DOMICILE

The domicile of the infant, instead of the residence of the petitioner, determines the question of jurisdiction, though when both are in the confines of one state the jurisdiction is usually either in the county where the child is living or where the petitioner resides. A court in one state has no jurisdiction over an individual in another state, and after the guardianship relationship is established the domicile of the ward follows that of the guardian. The guardianship is good only in the state where the appointment is made unless it is recognized as a matter of comity by a court in another state. Sometimes, in order to settle a large estate or to provide for a

[8] Adams' Appeal from Probate Court, 38 Conn. 304.

runaway child who has gone into another state, a temporary guardianship is granted in view of the one already existing in the state of the domicile. In a case which involved a runaway girl from New Hampshire a probate judge in Massachusetts recognized the appointment of a New Hampshire guardian and granted her a temporary guardianship in Massachusetts. The guardian then had the right to bring her ward back to her own state.

THE WELFARE OF THE CHILD

The court has the right to restrain a guardian from moving a ward to another state if it is not for the best interests of the child. An example of this often arises in divorce cases when the custody is given to a third party. If it is not for the best welfare of the child to live a part of the time with either one parent or the other who is outside the state, the guardian with the approval of the court can refuse to allow this. This is analogous to the situation which arises when a person, who is without legal authority, has acted in the place of a guardian for many years and is suddenly confronted by a parent who appears to claim the child. We are all familiar with a situation of this sort, and the decisions of the courts have not been uniform. Sometimes the court gives the custody to the parent, because of the parental tie, and at other times to the person who has given years of care, motivated by love for the child. The decisions hinge on a consideration of what is best for the child.

DUTIES AND POWERS OF THE GUARDIAN

While guardianship may entail a financial responsibility, this is not necessarily true. A guardian may have control of the person only and be under no personal obligation to support the ward. But if the child has an estate, the guardian acting under the court has the responsibility of administering the estate also. The following illustrates this. An illegitimate child who was born in Massachusetts was brought to New Hampshire for care, as his mother's residence before her death was in that state. The father wished to adopt his son, but as his wife would not consent, he became guardian and provided for the boy's support in a boarding home. Later when the father was killed in an accident another guardian was appointed to look after the boy and administer the estate which his father had willed to him. This was used by the guardian for the child's board, care, and education until he was old enough to look after himself.

A guardian's first duty, like that of a parent, is to maintain and educate his ward in a manner appropriate to the ward's income; or, if the child has no estate, to plan otherwise for his maintenance and education. As a guardian is not liable personally for the support of his ward, the law implies no promise that he will pay for the necessities of life. One state holds that the guardian has no authority to make advances from his own means for the ward and if he does this he cannot recover when the ward becomes of age.[4] Decisions are not in agreement as to whether or not a guardian may collect for board and clothing if the child is taken into the guardian's own family.

While a guardian has a great deal of discretionary power, he is expected to use judgment, as well as care and honesty, in the management of the estate which he holds as trustee for his ward. The court is primarily interested in protecting the rights of the child or ward and the

[4] Decisions of the Supreme Court in Virginia.

statutes prescribe definite conduct which the guardian must follow. If he fails in any respect, the court can remove him. A guardian is required to give a bond with security for the faithful performance of his duties, and even when there is no property a nominal bond is usually necessary. A guardian and his sureties are responsible for all the property coming into his hands, so there must be a fair and just appraisal of the estate by a disinterested party. He has the right to invest, to lease real estate during the minority of the ward, and sometimes to sell this as well as personal property with the permission of the court. He must keep the real property in repair and pay the taxes on it, and if some of this property is in another state he usually has to file a certificate of appointment as guardian before he can transfer the property. Many states prescribe how the funds of a ward can be invested and by this means try to insure against speculation. In states which are without such statutes investments in government bonds and real estate mortgages have the sanction of the courts. A guardian is responsible for losses from investments even though he acted with good intentions, but if there are benefits instead of losses the ward may claim these. If the guardian occupies property of the ward he is liable for rent, also for any depreciation caused by his lack of care. If he sells real estate the deed must conform to the statutory requirements and must show the guardian's authority; sometimes the guardian must have the consent of the court as well.

TRUST FUNDS

A guardian, like a trustee, has no right to mingle the ward's funds with his own in a bank account, but if he does this the law is on the side of the ward and looks upon it as a trust fund which the ward can follow and claim wherever he can find it. This includes the original property or any that has been substituted. There have been a great many decisions involving the misappropriation of funds and some courts have held that if the guardian acted in good faith and only intended to benefit the ward, by putting money in his own name, he should not be held responsible. If the trust fund happens to be real property, formerly the guardian could not buy it from the ward. This is an application of the principle that an agent cannot purchase the principal's property for himself, for there is an implication that the chance for fraud is great. At the present time these transactions are voidable and dependent upon the action of the infant upon reaching majority when he can enforce his rights. The court does not look upon gifts from the ward to the guardian with favor, because there is a presumption of undue influence, though it is possible to show that the gift was voluntary.

TERMINATION OF GUARDIANSHIP

The court has the power to remove a guardian for any one of several causes which show bad faith or neglect of duty in the management of the estate and are contrary to the interests of the ward. The guardianship is terminated by the death of either the guardian or the ward, by the ward reaching majority, by the marriage of a female ward, and, in some states, by the marriage of a female guardian, and, finally, by the removal of the guardian by the court, or by resignation for a reason which the court will accept. A court always requires a final accounting when the guardianship terminates, and many courts and the United States Government require a yearly accounting. Very often the court passes the yearly accounts because there is no one to question them, as the ward is not of sufficient age and discretion to do so. If the ward on attaining his majority discovers that his guardian has neglected his interests or acted in a fraudulent manner in administering the trust, he can apply to the proper court, to have the account opened and re-examined.

APPRENTICESHIP

In England there was another group of persons, usually minors, who were bound under a relationship which in some ways was similar to guardianship and was included in the group of family relationships, together with husband and wife, and guardian and ward. This was apprenticeship, but it can no longer be considered a family relationship as the character of the master and servant relation has changed from one of status to one of contract, due to the changes in the economic and social conditions which caused it to develop. Before there was manufacturing on a large scale the necessary trades and arts were carried on by skilled artisans, either in their own homes or in small shops, and children were apprenticed to masters who could teach them a trade. The apprentice served the master, who was entitled to any money which the apprentice earned while working for others during the apprenticeship, and in return the master gave maintenance and training. Statutes in most states provide for apprenticeship and prescribe a method of binding out, either by the parent or by a public official, such as the overseer of poor or selectman, if the father is dead.

Though the original purpose was to provide a useful trade for a minor if he could not obtain this otherwise, the developments in modern life have made this type of training unnecessary and undesirable and apprenticeship is not practiced very generally. Both relationships carry with them a responsibility and should not be entered into without consideration of the obligation involved, or without determination to fulfill the trust.

9.

ADOPTION

ADOPTION is the legal process which establishes the relationship of parent and child between persons not so related by birth. According to the usual understanding of the lay person, it is the act of taking the child of another into one's family and treating him as one's own.

ADOPTION AN ANCIENT PRACTICE

The practice of adoption was sanctioned by early civilizations as a method of caring for children. For some reason it was never accepted as a part of the common law of England and so could not become the practice in this country without statutory provision, except in states which based their legal systems upon the Roman law.[1] The social and legal aspects have not developed side by side, but it is difficult to adhere strictly to one or the other in any consideration of this alliance which can spell so much happiness or disaster. Though it is possible in most states to adopt an adult, this is not a usual practice and we think of the term as applicable only to children and usually to very young children.

[1] Louisiana and Texas.

EARLY LEGISLATION

The first adoption law in this country was passed in Massachusetts in 1851 and, like early statutes in other states, put emphasis on the rights of inheritance and the legal privileges involved, instead of upon the social aspects of the relationship.

ADOPTION BY DEED

The simplest form of adoption proceeding is by deed, which is certified and filed as a transfer of property is filed. This process completes the transfer of the child from one set of parents to another. Statutory provision still allows this procedure in Louisiana for children over eighteen and for adults. While it may have established inheritance rights for a child, it is a question whether or not it ever took away all parental rights without the written consent of the parent or parents. Certain rulings on appeal have held that, without the consent of the parents, adoption by deed would hold for the inheritance of property but would not stand as an adoption otherwise. Statutory provisions have now practically done away with this form of procedure.

JURISDICTION

The general practice is to require a formal proceeding before a judicial tribunal, which is usually the probate or orphans' court. Probably because the first conception of adoption was allied with inheritance and support, it was placed under the jurisdiction of the court having to do with property rights. Where more socialized aspects of adoption have permeated the law, the family courts or even the juvenile courts have attained jurisdiction. The great danger in placing the jurisdiction in the probate court is that as this court has jurisdiction of property, which is one of the most complicated and technical divisions of the law, the adoption procedure is likely to be rigid, with little consciousness of the social factors involved. There may be no machinery for the social investigation, which should be an important part of every adoption proceeding. On the other hand, there is ground for the belief that the jurisdiction in adoption cases should be kept in the court which historically had to do with matters of probate instead of placing it in the court that has to do with the delinquencies of parents or children.

The court having jurisdiction of adoption may be a county probate court, some other county or circuit court, a juvenile court, or a court covering a larger or smaller unit than a county court.

The practice which governs the jurisdiction of the person is quite varied. Some states require that the petition shall be brought where the petitioner resides,[2] a few provide that jurisdiction shall follow the residence of the child,[3] and all the other states provide that the petition may be brought either where the petitioner or the child resides. This gives a nonresident the privilege of adopting a child in the state where the child lives.

Some of these states, by implication, allow a nonresi-

---

[2] These are California, Delaware, Florida, Idaho, Michigan, Minnesota, Montana, Nebraska, Nevada, North Dakota, Oklahoma, Rhode Island, Utah, Virginia, West Virginia, Wisconsin.

[3] Arizona, Georgia, and Indiana.

dent to adopt a child because there is no residential or jurisdictional restriction which excludes a nonresident from petitioning. Adopting parents sometimes prefer to have the legal procedure and records where the child lives, for if the petitioners live in another state they think their friends are less likely to have access to records which will give information adverse to the interests of the child. From a legal standpoint, however, the best procedure seems to be that the residence of the adoptive parents should be the place of jurisdiction.

Some states provide that if a child has been abandoned or for some other reason has become a ward of an institution, the court where the institution is located shall have the right to grant adoption. The consent of the institution is required also.

CHANGE OF BIRTH CERTIFICATE

To eliminate any difficulty about records, five states [4] make provision in the adoption law for the court to send a report of the adoption to the state registrar of vital statistics, and he is authorized to change the birth certificate so that the adoptive parents appear as the natural parents. Other states make similar provision in the vital statistics law, and six states provide for registration but do not require a change on the birth certificate.

PARTIES TO THE ADOPTION

There are at least three parties or sets of parties concerned in the adoption proceeding which is started, as we have seen, by means of a petition to the proper court.

[4] Alabama, Delaware, Louisiana, Maine, and North Carolina.

They are the party or parties wishing to adopt the child, the natural parent or parents or guardian, and the child. While there are restrictions concerning the petitioners, these largely refer to age, reputation, and certain legal formalities and not to the motives underlying the act.

For instance, the state law of Massachusetts specifies that a person of full age may adopt a person younger than himself, and some states specify that the person who is adopting must be at least ten years older than the one who is to be adopted.[5] Louisiana, Montana, Nevada, and Texas do not allow the adoption of a person who has the blood of another race, such as the Negro or Mongolian, by a white person. Most statutes provide that if the person who wishes to adopt another is married the husband or wife must join in the petition or at least consent to the arrangement. As they will both become the parents of the child this seems the only logical policy. In addition to this, many statutes specify that the petition shall include the names and addresses of the petitioners; the name and age of the child and the name by which he is to be known; also the names and address of the natural parents and any information which is known about them, except that if the child is illegitimate a few states, including Illinois, Massachusetts, and New York, do not allow any reference to illegitimacy in the petition or the decree.

As adoption severs the child's relationship to its own parents, it is only right that the parents should have every opportunity to appear in the interests of the child and consent to the change of status. Therefore, unless a parent is mentally incompetent or morally unfit, or has

---

[5] California, Montana, Nevada, New Jersey, New Mexico, North Dakota, Oklahoma, South Dakota, and Utah. Idaho requires that the person adopting must be fifteen years older than the person adopted.

lost custody through divorce, or the child has been placed under the control of some child-caring agency by the court, consent of the parents is required by statute in all states. If the child is illegitimate, the consent of the mother only is required. If the parents are dead or are incompetent, and the child has no guardian, a state department or other agency serving as *guardian ad litem* or next friend can represent the interests of the child and give consent to the adoption.[6] All but eight states also require the consent of a child to his adoption if he is over a specific age, which is usually fourteen, though in California, Idaho, Montana, and New Mexico it is twelve, and in North Dakota, and in Michigan, under certain circumstances, it is ten.

In many states the law specifies that the petitioner must appear in person; also, the parents or guardian must appear unless they live outside the state, or for some other good reason are unable to be present. This requirement may be waived in that case, but even then the consent must be shown in writing. In most instances, it is shown by the petition which is signed by the natural parent or parents. Sometimes adopting parents do not like to have the natural parent or parents know who is adopting the child—especially if the child is illegitimate—and the signature of the mother without this knowledge is legal in some states.

SOCIAL INVESTIGATION

If there is any branch of legal procedure dealing with the lives of human beings which needs the aid of a social

[6] Alabama, California, Delaware, Kentucky, Minnesota, North Dakota, and Wisconsin place this authority in the state department, while in New Jersey and Ohio the state department or an agency serving as next friend can give consent.

investigation it is adoption. The court should concern itself mainly with the welfare of the child and demand a searching inquiry into the fitness of the adopting parents.

The growing interest in the welfare of the adopted child has been reflected in recent legislation, and about half of the states now authorize a social investigation—either by a state agency, such as the Department of Welfare, or some other state department; or by some person or agency appointed by the court having jurisdiction.[7] The trend is increasingly toward greater protection of children and a more careful examination of the home to which the child is going. State statutes specify that a judge shall be satisfied that the petitioner is of good moral character, of reputable standing in the community, and of ability to properly maintain and educate the child whom he wishes to adopt, and also that it is for the best interest of the child to be adopted. This is probably as far as the language of the law can be expected to go, and yet there are more subtle aspects of this age-old social institution which are outside the realm of legal phraseology but which affect the social side of adoption acutely. An eminent child psychiatrist has said: "Who is to appear in the interest of the child and inquire for him, 'Why do these people want me? What kind of people are they? Are they thinking of having someone to support them in their old age? Or do they want something

[7] These are Alabama, Arizona, Arkansas, California, Delaware, Iowa, Kansas, Kentucky, Louisiana, Massachusetts, Michigan, Minnesota, New Jersey, New Mexico, New York, North Carolina, North Dakota, Ohio, Oregon, Rhode Island, South Dakota, Texas, Virginia, Wisconsin. The court may at its discretion request an investigation in Maine by the State Bureau of Social Welfare, and in New Hampshire the probate court may ask the probation officer or the State Department of Welfare to make an investigation. In Pennsylvania the court may ask some person or agency to investigate and verify the facts set forth in the petition and such other facts as the court wishes.

to play with for the moment? What have they done to demonstrate that they are capable of bringing up a child? Has it ever occurred to them that I might not have chosen them had I had any say in the matter? How old are these prospective parents of mine? Let them consider how old they will be when I am in need of counsel and advice in early adolescence.' "[8]

Only when the emotional urges and motives of the petitioner as well as the emotional needs of the child are considered can there be a thorough and sympathetic understanding of the whole situation. To how great depths the social investigation penetrates depends upon the facilities at hand for the study of the individual and also upon the personality of the one who makes the investigation. Every children's agency is familiar with the results of ill-advised adoptions like the following:

A couple with one child had lost three children at birth. After the loss of the third child they were advised by their family physician to adopt a child who was born of an unmarried mother at the same time and in the same hospital as their own child. Without knowing anything about the antecedents of this child they took him, intending to adopt him. Actually they never went through with the legal procedure though he went by their name. This was a bad situation from the beginning for they were then in no emotional state to undertake the care of this child. The later illness and death of the foster father made family life impossible, and three years spent in rather rigid schools did not help to solve the problems of this boy. At the age of eleven he was accepted by a child-caring agency in the state where he was born—a

[8] Douglas A. Thom, *Normal Youth and Its Everyday Problems*, pp. 35–37.

very unhappy little boy, having many deep-seated behavior problems, and badly needing psychiatric help. If any investigation had been made by a children's agency, this situation could have been avoided, as the parents' emotional instability would have been discovered.

TRIAL PERIOD

Even when every precaution has been taken before placement, social agencies recognize that a trial period is essential in order to be quite sure that the relation is going to be a satisfactory one. Many states have seen the wisdom of this and have provided by statute for a trial period before the decree is granted, though in some states this may be waived at the discretion of the judge.[9] The trial period varies in the different states from six months to one year. During this time supervision is essential, for otherwise the trial period would be of no value.

A little girl was taken from a county institution, and was adopted without any investigation or any waiting period to prove the stability of the arrangement. Before the child was five she was the victim of the most distressing sex abuse. Supervision of this home would have shown the dangers even if the necessary investigation had not been made before the placement.

The importance of a waiting period is closely allied

---

[9] The states which provide for a trial period are: Alabama, Arizona, Arkansas, Delaware, District of Columbia, Georgia, Iowa, Kansas, Louisiana, Massachusetts, Minnesota, New Jersey, New Mexico, New York, North Carolina, North Dakota, Ohio, Rhode Island, South Dakota, Texas, Virginia, Wisconsin. In Maine the court may at its discretion require a residence in the home of the petitioners, and the child may be placed under the supervision of an agency; in Vermont the adoption is not final until one year after filing the petition and the court holds the case open during that time.

with jurisdiction, for surely when a period of waiting is a part of the required procedure of every state, supervision will be easier if the parties are within the jurisdiction of the court. This supervision is often given now by children's agencies upon a reciprocal basis, and a report is sent to the agency, which will be responsible for the adoption. For example, a child born in New Hampshire was taken into the family of her aunt in Connecticut, after an investigation of that home by a Connecticut agency, with the understanding that the child should be adopted at the end of a year if conditions were still satisfactory. The Connecticut agency supervised during the period but the adoption was consummated in New Hampshire.

RECORD OF ADOPTION

Usually a judicial decree of adoption, like any other decision, is a matter of public record but a few states recognize the unusual nature of the proceeding and provide by statute that the records shall be open only to the parties in interest, their attorneys, or to an authorized state department, unless there is an order from the court.

COMPLETE CHANGE OF LEGAL STATUS

When an adoption decree has been made by the court there are certain rights and obligations which affect all the parties to the relationship. The legal status of the child is completely changed. The natural parents are deprived by law of all legal rights to the child; these are transferred to the adopting parents, whose rights and duties are the same as if the child had been born to them. The first result of this relationship to the child is the right to bear the name of the adopting parents. It is as much his legal name as if it has been conferred by birth; and he is entitled to support, care, and education the same as an own child. The adopting parents, on the other hand, have the right of custody and the right to the child's services and earnings during minority. Both parents and children usually have reciprocal rights of inheritance, though this is not always true. As we have seen, in early times the desire to have an heir was one motive underlying adoption. Though in most states an adopted child inherits equally with an own child from the parents' estate, it has generally been held that the adopted child cannot inherit through the parents from their ancestors or kindred; so if there is an own child in the family of the adoptive parents, both children inherit equally from the parents, unless there is a will which provides otherwise, or a statute which specifies that only heirs of the body may inherit; but the adopted child will not inherit from grandparents who die after the adoption took place.

In a Massachusetts case it was held that an adopted child had the right of inheritance as against an uncle and aunt in the property of a sister by adoption.[10] This decision was on the ground that the adopted child would take the same share in the parents' estate as if he had been born to them and would stand in the same relation to legal descendants of the parents but to no other kindred. The decisions in Washington, Iowa, and New Jersey have been according to the same interpretation of the statutes. Twelve states provide that an adopted child does not lose the right to inherit also from his natural parents.[11]

---

[10] Stearns v. Allen, 183 Mass. 404.

[11] Alabama, Arkansas, Colorado, Florida, Kentucky, Maine, Massachusetts, New Jersey, New York, Ohio, Texas, and West Virginia provide this.

ANNULMENT OF ADOPTION

The relationship of adoption is unlike guardianship in that it is a permanent one. But mistakes may be made and conditions may change, and so several states have enacted laws to protect both the child and the adoptive parents from conditions arising after adoption. Some states provide for annulment if the adoptive parents violate their agreement for proper care and treatment of the child. In Minnesota if within five years the child has developed certain defects—such as feeblemindedness, insanity, epilepsy, or venereal disease,—from conditions existing prior to the adoption and then unknown to the adoptive parents, the decree may be annulled. The law in Alabama, Arkansas, California, Iowa, Missouri, Ohio, Utah, and Wisconsin is similar to this.

In a few states the natural parents and the child are protected against untrue statements made by the adoptive parents at the time of the adoption, and the court can revoke the adoption if any of the material allegations were untrue. Often the most practical way to sever the relationship in an undesirable adoption is to proceed as with a child who is living with its natural parents and either prove through juvenile court proceedings that the child is neglected or petition for guardianship of the child.

ADOPTION BY ACKNOWLEDGMENT

Throughout this chapter we have considered legal adoption only and the statutory procedure which has been established in the various states. In connection with this it should be mentioned that in eight states—namely,

California, Idaho, Montana, Nevada, North Dakota, Oklahoma, South Dakota, and Utah—the father of an illegitimate child can adopt it by making a public acknowledgment that he is the father, and receiving it into his family with the consent of his wife, if he is married, and otherwise treating it as if it were legitimate. This is in contrast to the rule that the child, who has been accepted by foster parents without judicial procedure, is not actually an adopted child in the eyes of the law, though the foster parents look upon him as their child. Because there has been a good deal of this sort of placement by parents and well-intentioned persons, some states have placed restrictions on the transfer of children by their parents without an order of the court or the State Department of Welfare.

RESTRICTIVE LAWS RELATIVE TO ADOPTION

Laws have become more restrictive as they relate to the policy of maternity hospitals and child-caring institutions, from which many children are taken for adoption. However, some very unsavory practices still exist. A well-known judge of a juvenile and domestic relations court is authority for the statement that "Prior to 1922 it was the common practice in Virginia for commercial maternity homes virtually to sell babies born in their institutions.[12] A fee was charged to the expectant mother when she was admitted to the home. A few weeks after the birth of the baby she was permitted to leave the home and her baby upon signing her consent to an adoption paper which did not name the adopting parent. Married couples, or individuals, who desired to adopt a baby

[12] James Hoge Ricks, *Legal Aspects of Adoption*, p. 4.

would come to the maternity home, look over the babies, as though they were so many puppies, select the one whose appearance appealed to them, pay a fee or 'donation' of $50, $100 or more and, with the aid of the matron or superintendent of the home, secure from a local court immediate approval of the adoption, without any inquiry as to the moral fitness or financial responsibility of the adopters and with no examination of the baby to determine its physical or mental condition."

THE RESPONSIBILITY OF THE STATE

Undesirable conditions existed in other states and still exist to some extent today. However, the feeling that adoption is a responsibility of the state is becoming increasingly strong and legislation relating to it shows a gradual change from a transaction that was primarily contractual to a procedure which places emphasis on the social well-being of the child. There is still much to be done, nevertheless, before every child will have adequate protection, which is possible only when there is a complete social investigation; a trial period under supervision before the decree becomes final; a provision for annulment if the welfare of the child demands it; and, finally, a provision that some department of the state—preferably the State Department of Welfare or Division of Guardianship—shall pass upon all adoptions and supervise social agencies or persons who are active in bringing about this important relationship.[18]

---

[18] It should be understood that adoption laws are changing very rapidly and that every year additional states make provision for the protection of their children along the lines of the best social thinking of the day.

10.

SECURITY LEGISLATION

THE word *security*, as it applies to the economic, social, and emotional relations of human beings, has crept into our thinking and living in the past few years with tremendous rapidity. Now through an orderly plan of legislation termed the Federal Social Security Act its application has broadened, and by means of legal protection an attempt has been made to substitute a feeling of safety and assurance in place of the fear of unemployment, apprehension for a dependent old age, and certain distresses of childhood. If we say that social legislation relates to specific laws which affect the happiness and welfare of individuals by bringing about a better adjustment of the conditions under which they are living, then this Act initiates a program which shows great progress in social legislative planning and which affects millions of men, women, and children. This program represents a great change in the thinking of the American people. The depression, following the World War, which threw millions out of work, placed little value on the unemployment of older men, and swept away the savings of a lifetime, was partially responsible for it and brought about a realization of the necessity of legislation which would provide "safeguards against misfortunes which cannot be wholly eliminated in this man-made world of ours."[1] These conditions led up to the appointment of a Committee on Economic Security and from their recommendations, following an intensive study and investigation, the program developed which, with many changes and revisions, became the present Social Security Act. This program aims to bring about security for individuals and for the family.

THE CHANGE IN POPULATION

Because of the lower birth rate and an increased proportion of the aged to the whole population, adequate care for this group became of primary importance. The men, who had been the breadwinners, and the women, who had helped to develop character and implant standards of right living in growing families, suddenly found conditions changed when the men became too old to longer be necessary or useful in the economic world. All were swept along in a maelstrom of defeat, insecurity, and dependence upon children or relatives scarcely able to help them, or upon the public relief rolls. In 1890 only 3 per cent of the total population were sixty-five years of age or more but by 1930 this group had increased to 5.4 per cent. In 1890 only 26.2 per cent were not gainfully employed, but by 1930 this number had reached 41.0 per cent, and by 1934 three-quarters of a million of aged people were on relief.

PROTECTION FOR THE AGED

The security legislation provides two types of protection for the aged in its program. These are federal aid to

[1] President Roosevelt in a message to Congress in June 1934.

the states for old age assistance, or pensions paid on a matching basis with the states, and old age insurance, or benefits on an annuity basis paid entirely by the Federal Government. There were precedents for the system of grants in aid under which the first type of assistance is administered, for there had been federal land grants and grants to promote higher education; there had been also grants to the states on a matching basis for fire protection, agricultural expansion, vocational education, and highway construction; and through the Public Health programs there had been grants for the prevention of social diseases, and for the care of mothers and infants. From a legal standpoint this system had been declared constitutional.

Old Age Assistance.— The old age assistance which is administered by the states in coöperation with the Federal Government is granted on the basis of individual need. The original act provided that the Federal Government would contribute one-half of any pension which was not more than $30 a month, thereby paying $15 as its share. If the pension was less than $30, it would pay one-half of the sum, but if more than $30 the state had to pay the difference between $15 and the total amount paid. The amendment of 1939 does not specifically change the amount of assistance given to needy aged persons but increases the amount which the Federal Government will pay toward the cost of this assistance. The share of the Federal Government may now be up to $20 of each $40 paid to an individual instead of up to $15 of each $30 paid by the state, as previously provided. The final decision as to the amount of each grant rests with the states, however, and must be in accordance with the state law.

The Federal Government also provides an additional 5 per cent of the total grant which may be used for administrative purposes or for assistance to individuals, or for both. In order to receive old age assistance funds from the Federal Government the states must conform to certain conditions as to age and residence, as well as to approved administrative policies. At first the age requirement could be, and in a few states was, as high as seventy, but by 1940 the age of eligibility was fixed at sixty-five. If it is lower than that the Government will not contribute. Individuals who wish to have this assistance must be living in private homes or private institutions, with residence in the state for five of the nine preceding years, and with one year of continuous residence preceding the application. The states must have plans which are statewide and are mandatory and must furnish the required proportion of the funds. The responsibility of the local community is stressed and part of the financial burden may be transferred to other sub-divisions of the state, but the state must retain the responsibility for administration and supervision, either directly or indirectly, through its smaller governmental units. The states must accept the approved methods of administration which the Social Security Board requires and must report to that board. If a state collects funds from the estate of a person who received a pension, these must be shared equally with the Federal Government. Grants from the Federal Government are made quarterly in advance, upon the basis of estimates made by the state authorities, and if the estimate is incorrect the amount is deducted or added in the next allowance. This relieves the state of the burden of carrying the current expenses. When an individual or a married couple applies for this type of aid, the social worker makes a thorough investigation as to whether there are children who can help the parents, as to the valuation of any property owned by the applicant, and as to the existence of insurance or bank accounts. When Mr. and Mrs. Smith applied for aid, it was found that Mr. Smith had always been thrifty and hard working and that he had bought real estate when he was able to save; but this had depreciated in value and their only child was married to a man who had been out of work for a long time. A careful checking of the income and needs of the couple showed that they should have an old age assistance grant.

Old Age Benefits.— Along with the plan of assistance grants to the needy aged is the other form of protection; namely, old age insurance benefits, which are paid directly to the individual by the Government, not on the basis of need but on the basis of the individual's work record. The intention is to prevent future dependence of the aged who are in the low income groups. This is contributory while the other is noncontributory, and it represents a long view ahead, while old age assistance takes care only of the emergency. The concept of old age insurance is not new, as efforts were being made by the middle of the nineteenth century toward a workable noncontributory plan in at least three foreign countries. Such a plan has existed in Germany since 1891. Since the World War, fifteen countries, including France, Great Britain, and Italy, have established a contributory old age system. In these countries the coverage is more inclusive, sometimes including agricultural and domestic workers; but the benefits paid are smaller than the individual amounts paid under the Social Security Act in the United States.

When the original act was passed in 1935 Congress recognized that changes would be necessary after a period of administrative experience; so the Social Security Board was authorized to study the act and recommend changes to the President and Congress. Many of these recommendations were accepted by Congress in 1939 and are now embodied in the law. While some of the changes are minor ones, there are major modifications in the law which relates to old age benefits. Briefly, these refer to the groups covered under the act, to the formula for computing the amount of the benefit, and to the change in the tax levy on both the employer and employee.

The original act applied only to persons in commerce and industry. Agricultural laborers were excluded, and so were those in domestic service, maritime service, and the service of government, whether federal, state, or local. Workers in fields of charity, science, literature, and education and those employed by non-profit-making organizations were also ineligible under the act. As revised, the act has been extended to include employees of national banks, employees of building and loan associations, and employees of state banks which are members of the Federal Reserve System, employees in maritime service on American vessels, and workers who are over sixty-five. There has been a redefining of terms, and agricultural labor has been extended to cover certain services which are closely allied to farming and which were not previously excluded. Domestic service has been defined as service in a private home, local college club, fraternity or sorority. It is estimated that more than a million additional persons are eligible for old age benefits under the 1939 revision of the act. Other groups will probably become eligible through future amendments.

TAXES TO FINANCE OLD AGE BENEFITS

Old age benefits are financed by taxes on payrolls and wages. These taxes are shared equally by employers and employees, and under the first law the combined tax amounted to 2 per cent a year from 1937 to 1939 inclusive, and then increased at the rate of 1 per cent at three-year intervals through 1948. At that time both employer and employee would be paying 2.5 per cent, or a combined tax of 5 per cent. In 1949 the combined tax of employer and employee was to become 6 per cent and continue at that rate.

Under the revision the taxes for three years, namely, from 1940 through 1942, do not increase as originally planned but are "frozen" at 1 per cent. The schedule of the original law becomes effective after January 1, 1943. It provides for an increase to 2 per cent in 1943, 2.5 per cent in 1946, and to a maximum of 3 per cent in 1949 for both employers and employees. This change was made as a result of the criticism levelled at this part of the Social Security Act, and the criticism, in turn was due to the accumulation of the very large reserve fund. The effect of this change is to diminish the growth of the reserve fund. The first monthly benefit payment was made in 1940 instead of 1942, as originally scheduled.

Under the original law the benefits were computed on a basis of the individual's total accumulative wages after December 1936 and before he became sixty-five years of age, but under the new law the benefits are computed on the basis of the individual's average monthly wage from covered employment. To carry the comparison a little further, $2,000 was the minimum amount considered for accumulated wages over a five-year period, and $3,000 was the largest amount considered as wages in any one year. If the total amount earned over a period of years was more than $3,000, the amount of the old age monthly benefit was one-half of 1 per cent of the first $3,000, plus one-twelfth of 1 per cent of any additional amount up to $45,000, and one twenty-fourth of 1 per cent of any amount over $45,000. To illustrate this concretely: if Mr. Brown earned $100 a month over a five-year period from 1937 to 1942 and then retired at sixty-five, the benefit he would receive on retiring would be computed on $6,000, or his accumulated wages, and would be $17.50 per month. Under the new plan the benefit is determined on Mr. Brown's earnings as follows: 40 per cent on the first $50 of average monthly wages, plus 10 per cent of his average wages over $50 and up to $250, and an additional 1 per cent of his basic benefit for every year in which he earns at least $200 in covered employment. Instead of $17.50, Mr. Brown will receive $26.25.

SUPPLEMENTARY AND SURVIVOR BENEFITS

The new law considers the needs and security of the worker's family and provides for supplementary benefits to wives and dependent children, under certain conditions, as well as for monthly benefits to survivors. A knowledge of the qualifications which are necessary in order to receive these benefits is dependent upon an understanding of the terms "fully insured" and "currently insured," which were not used in the original act.

In order to be fully insured the worker must have "quarters of coverage" equal to half the number of quarters after 1936 (or his twenty-first birthday if it is later) and before the quarter in which he became sixty-five or died; but in no case less than six quarters of coverage. When a worker has forty quarters of coverage he is fully insured, regardless of his employment thereafter. To be currently insured the worker must have had at least six quarters of coverage in the three years preceding the quarter in which he died. The family of the fully insured worker can receive supplementary benefits or survivor's benefits, while a currently insured worker's family can receive only survivor's benefits for dependent children or survivor's benefits for widows with dependent children in their care. If a worker is "fully insured" or "currently insured" a lump sum death benefit is paid when there is no survivor entitled to monthly benefits.

To continue with the illustration of the Brown family: —as Mr. Brown is fully insured Mrs. Brown at sixty-five years of age will receive a supplementary benefit equal to one-half of her husband's monthly benefit, unless she is entitled to a monthly old age benefit as large as, or larger than, the supplementary amount. Mrs. Brown will therefore receive $13.12 in addition to the $26.25 which her husband receives. If there is one dependent child under eighteen who is going to school, the child will receive the same amount as his mother, and the total income of the family will be $52.50.[2] If the worker is sixty-five and the mother is younger, the dependent child only can receive the supplementary benefit, for the mother will not be eligible until she is sixty-five.

Formerly there was no provision for monthly benefits for the survivors, though there was a provision that the estate of an individual should receive a lump sum payment

---

[2] Though this would be possible according to the terms of the law, it probably would not happen in actual practice for it is extremely unlikely that a woman sixty-five years of age would have a child of sixteen, or even eighteen, unless by adoption.

equal to 3.5 per cent of the total wages earned after 1936 and until the death of the individual, if he died before he became sixty-five. Under the present rule if a qualified worker dies after 1939, the widow, if she is sixty-five or if she has children dependent on her, will receive a monthly benefit of three-fourths of the worker's benefit rate, and again each unmarried dependent child under eighteen will receive one-half of the worker's benefit rate. If there is no widow or dependent child, each dependent parent who is sixty-five or over will receive one-half of the worker's benefit rate.

For example, to again take $100 as the average monthly wage on which the worker will receive a monthly benefit of $26.25, the widow will receive $19.69 if she is sixty-five or if she is caring for a dependent child, and each dependent child will receive $13.12. Each dependent parent will receive $13.12 if there is no wife or child surviving. If there are no survivors who are entitled to monthly benefits, a lump sum payment is made. The amount is six times the monthly benefit. This will go to a parent who is not dependent or for funeral expenses.

REMOVAL OF THE "STOP DATE"

Formerly a worker must retire on reaching sixty-five in order to receive monthly benefits and anything he earned after that time could not be counted toward benefits, but now a worker may work after he is sixty-five and continue to build up wage credits and increase the amounts of the benefits he will receive when he retires. Many who received a lump sum payment before the act was changed could still qualify under the amendments for monthly benefits beginning January 1, 1939, and the amount previously paid was deducted from the monthly benefits. A worker is entitled to a larger amount under the amendments than he would have been under the old plan. For example, if a man had been earning $100 a month for three years prior to December 31, 1939, when he became sixty-five he would receive 3.5 per cent of $3600, his total wages, or $126. Under the amended program the monthly benefit is computed on his average wage over the three-year period and will be $26.25 a month for the rest of his life. He does not collect any money until he retires under either plan, though if he is not working in covered employment but is earning $15 a month or less this does not count as working. The minimum monthly benefit which an individual can receive is $10; but if the total benefit payment of a worker and dependents is more than $20, it cannot exceed 80 per cent of his average monthly wage or twice his primary insurance benefit or $85, whichever is the least. Eighty-five dollars is the maximum monthly benefit.

INSURANCE FUND

Instead of the Old Age Reserve Account set up in the Treasury, there is an Old Age Survivors' Trust Fund. There is a board of three trustees—the Secretary of the Treasury, the Secretary of Labor, and the Chairman of the Social Security Board—which administers the funds.

UNEMPLOYMENT COMPENSATION

Security is provided for another group of individuals by unemployment compensation, which consists of cash payments at stated intervals to unemployed persons who are eligible. This plan has been tried and approved in other countries for many years. It began in Great Britain and Belgium in the latter part of the nineteenth century, and the first manifestation was through trade unions which provided regular allowances for those persons who became unemployed. This idea later spread to other countries, and municipalities in Switzerland and France began to supplement the allowances which were paid by the trade unions; finally about twenty-five years ago Great Britain developed a system of compulsory unemployment insurance, which has been taken as a basis for most of the systems which have subsequently developed.

The aim of the Social Security Act is to set up a system of unemployment compensation in the states and to administer this in coöperation with the federal government. The Act does not specify any type of law which is mandatory and any law which meets the needs of the individual state will be approved as long as it meets certain federal requirements. Within two years after the Security Act became effective all the states passed satisfactory laws. Perhaps this was due to the fact that under this coöperative system, unless a state had an approved law the entire tax on payrolls would go to the federal government, to be used by the government, and would not be available for unemployment benefits. The underlying principle of this compensation is that in good years provision should be made for times of unemployment; therefore, a fund should be built up to take care of benefits for those who are unemployed through no fault of their own, or those who are unemployed for a short period of time in changing from one employment to another.

TAXES ON PAYROLLS

The funds which are paid out in compensation are obtained from a federal tax on payrolls paid by employers who are engaged in any business which is not excluded under the law, if they employ the required number of persons, on one day in each of twenty different weeks of the year. This number of employees varies from one to eight or more in the different states. The federal taxes are collected by the Bureau of Internal Revenue and are based upon all the wages and salaries paid out during the previous year. Though an employer is allowed credit for contributions, in states which have a mandatory system of unemployment insurance, as a set-off on the federal tax levy on payrolls, this credit cannot exceed 90 per cent of the federal tax. This really means that if the state has an approved law the state taxes will be credited against the federal tax up to 90 per cent and will not be an added burden on the employers.

COVERAGE

As in old age insurance, certain people are excluded, and under the original act individuals employed in agricultural labor, domestic service in private homes, shipping on both American and foreign vessels, in service for the federal, state or local government, and in religious, charitable, educational, and non-profit organizations, were excluded. The coverage has been extended so that employees in national banks, building and loan associations, and certain other organizations will now be covered if the states wish it. The present law has redefined agricultural labor and domestic service and extended exclusions much as they have been extended under the old age benefits. Further exclusions which were not contained in the first act are: service in the employ of a foreign government or its instrumentalities; service in occupations covered by the Railroad Unemployment Compensation Act; certain services where the remuneration is nominal and for voluntary, fraternal and beneficiary associations; services for schools and colleges, by regular students; for hospitals, by internes and nurses in training; family employment; and services by newsboys under eighteen.

Though charitable and non-profit-making institutions and agencies are exempt from income taxes and usually from property taxes, the employees of these institutions are not exempt and these exclusions may be a questionable discrimination. Any state through its laws may include persons in any employment except that of the federal government, of other states, or service on navigable waters, but in the beginning most states have followed the exemptions of the federal law.

FEDERAL AND STATE LAWS

There are advantages to employers and to the states in this coöperative plan with the federal government: first, the states are relieved of the financial burden of administering the unemployment compensation laws; secondly, by the uniform tax the employers are relieved of the disadvantage of competing with states that do not have the same laws; and, finally, by the privilege of set-off for 90 per cent of the state taxes both the state and the employers are freed from the necessity of paying heavy federal taxes. The state laws must conform to certain regulations in order to be approved by the security board and must contain specific provisions for the establishment and maintenance of personnel standards on a merit basis in order to receive grants for administrative expenses. The state must also conform to the provisions concerning the manner and time for payment of the compensation; for the payment of funds to the Secretary of the Treasury; and for the use of money withdrawn from unemployment trust funds. There is also an important provision that a state cannot deny an individual compensation for refusing to work under certain conditions; for instance, if the position offered is vacant because of a strike or a labor dispute, if the wages, hours, or other conditions of work are less favorable to the individual than those prevailing in a similar locality, or if unfair conditions are imposed in return for employment. States may pass laws that specify the coverage, the length of the waiting period, the amount of benefits, and the length of time the benefits will be paid. The state laws show a wide variation in these respects. For instance, in nine states employers of four or more workers are included,[3] and in seven states employers of one or more employees are included.[4] The coverage is established by law and controls the eligibility of the workers in each state, so if the law includes only employers of eight or more the employees of concerns that employ less than that number are excluded from participation.

Amount of Compensation.— The amount of compensation for total unemployment is 50 per cent of the employee's wages in many states, but this is usually qualified by a $15 a week maximum. Some states provide for a minimum of $5.00 or $7.50 a week, and a few states place the minimum as low as $3.00. Under most state laws partial unemployment benefits will be paid when the

---

[3] California, Kentucky, Massachusetts, Maryland, New Hampshire, New York, Oregon, Rhode Island, and Louisiana.

[4] District of Columbia, Delaware, Minnesota, Montana, Pennsylvania, Arkansas, and Wyoming.

weekly wages for part time work are not greater than the benefit rate for total unemployment.

Waiting Period.—In some states two weeks of partial unemployment are counted as one week of total unemployment, but most states require the same waiting period for partial as for total unemployment benefits; in both instances it is cumulative, and does not have to be continuous, but may be for interrupted periods during the year and usually amounts to three weeks. Illness is a bar to the unemployment benefit because in that case unemployment is due to inability to work. Likewise if a worker is discharged for misconduct some states pay no benefits. In others the waiting period is increased. The benefits are paid for a definite period, varying from twelve to twenty weeks of the year. A few states provide for continued benefits on the basis of the length of employment, though the usual policy is that the benefit is limited in ratio to the length of employment, as one week of benefit to either three or four weeks of employment during the preceding year or two years. In New York State it is one week of benefit to fifteen days of employment.

Payment Controlled by State Laws.—In order that the reserve fund may accumulate, the Act provides that benefits shall not be paid until two years after the contributions are begun under the state law; so the time of the first payment varies and is dependent upon the time when the state law became operative. Wisconsin in 1934 was the first state to pass a mandatory unemployment compensation law, and benefits became payable in July, 1936. Plans are further varied in different states as to the burden of taxes. In some states the burden of taxes is entirely on the employer, while in more than half the states the contribution is shared by the employee paying a smaller per cent than the employer, usually 1 per cent, which is deducted from the wages by the employer. This is the method in effect in practically all European countries.

Federal Employment Offices.— Federal employment offices have been established to assist in administering this law, and any individual who is unemployed is expected to register immediately with the federal office. This office will arrange for payments during the waiting period and will assist the individual to contact a new job.

PROTECTION FOR OTHER GROUPS

Besides protection for the aged and the unemployed the Social Security Act provides safeguards for children and those handicapped physically or otherwise. This is done by means of aid to dependent children; maternal and child health services; aid to crippled children; child welfare services, especially in rural areas; vocational rehabilitation; aid to the blind; and extension of public health service. All these services relate to the family and affect the security and welfare of the child as the most important member of the family in a positive way by the provisions for health, education, and adequate employment of the parents, and in a less obvious manner when funds which should go for the care of children are used to help aged relatives.

Aid to Dependent Children.— In future planning, the welfare, health, and development of the child becomes a joint responsibility of parents, community, and state and federal government. The concepts that the best place for a child is his own home and that a mother's care is worth more to her family than her contribution from work outside the home have gained recognition through the years, so that many states have passed laws providing for Mothers' Aid or Mothers' Pensions. The first laws putting this into effect were passed in Illinois and Missouri in 1911, and by 1934 there were only two states that did not have a Mothers' Aid law.[5] While aid was at first limited to families in which the father had died, the law of twenty-one states had made it available to families in which the father had deserted, had been imprisoned or divorced, or was physically or mentally disabled. Actually a large percentage of children cared for under the provision were the children of widowed mothers. In the words of the law, "Under the Social Security Act a dependent child means a child under the age of sixteen who has been deprived of parental support or care by reason of the death, continued absence from home, or physical or mental incapacity of a parent." This is the definition that will probably be accepted in most states though it is not essential for the receipt of federal aid.

Allowances for the support of the family before the passage of the Security Act were small and inadequate in many states, and the administration of the aid was not uniform. Some states had excellent systems, but in others the benefit to the recipient was questionable as it was permissive rather than mandatory. The expense was borne largely by the county rather than the state and in some counties no grants were made though the group that was eligible had increased during the depression. Individual states had been wholly unprepared to meet the need and discontinued aid for lack of funds; the situation was made more serious by the fact that there were

[5] Georgia and South Carolina.

children in about 40 per cent of the families on relief. By means of aid to dependent children under the Social Security Act, standards of administration have been raised through supervision and allowances have been increased to meet the minimum needs of the family. By the terms of the Act, aid to dependent children can be given to a child "who is living with his father, mother, grandfather, grandmother, brother, sister, stepfather, stepmother, stepbrother, stepsister, uncle, or aunt, in a place of residence maintained by one or more of such relatives as his or their own home."

Many times families who were receiving mothers' aid under the old state laws now have an increased appropriation through the Security Act under aid to dependent children. For instance, Mr. C, who had always been a good provider, dropped dead in 1932, leaving five children, the oldest of whom was twelve years old. The mother tried to live with some of her relatives for a time and contributed to the family income by working outside the home. This became too much for her and she was granted an allowance which enabled her to have an apartment and to stay at home with her children. The Mothers' Aid visitor helped her fit up her new home and make out her budget. She also planned vacations for the children, and arranged for necessary medical attention. She has kept in touch with the children in school, and has seen the oldest boy graduate and go into a C.C.C. camp. This friendly service on a case-work basis continues on a copartnership basis, with the visitor acting as the agent of both the federal government and the state.

The federal government pays to the states which have satisfactorily filled the requirements a sum equal to one-half of the total amount expended to the families, but the sum paid for each child must not exceed $18 a month for the first child and $12 a month for the other children in the family. The government also pays one-half the cost of administration. The plan, to be acceptable, must be mandatory in all sub-divisions of the state, provide for financial participation by the state and for a state agency to administer or supervise the administration of the plan. The Social Security Board requires certain methods of procedure. No state plan shall deny eligibility to any child who has resided in a state for a year preceding the application, or whose mother has resided in a state for one year before the birth of the child born within the year preceding the application; no state which has refused a claim with respect to a dependent child can deny an opportunity for a fair hearing. The original plan was to have aid to dependent children under the supervision of the Children's Bureau, which has the supervision of other services to children, but it was finally placed with old age assistance and unemployment insurance under the security board. It will be seen that the federal government will contribute only $9.00 as a maximum in the case of a dependent child while it will reimburse one-half of the maximum of $40 a month to persons entitled to old age assistance. It seems unfortunate that dependent children do not receive a larger grant.

Services for Children.—Three programs of federal and state participation were placed directly under the supervision of the Children's Bureau of the Department of Labor, and this Bureau was given the responsibility of working out plans of operation and administration relating to maternal and child health services, services for crippled children, and child welfare services. In all of these groups particular emphasis is placed on programs which are to be carried on in rural areas, because in many states such services were lacking entirely or the need was inadequately met through state or private agencies.

Maternal and Child Health Services.—Maternal and child health services relating to mothers and infants are a revival of the Shepard-Towner Act which was in effect from 1921 to 1928 and was accepted in all but three states. During the time of its operation infant mortality was reduced but the rate of maternal mortality was not lowered perceptibly during the seven-year period. Most states were not able to carry on a constructive program, as indicated by the record that twenty-three states had less than $10,000 for maternal and child health work by 1934, fourteen states had less than $3,000, fourteen states between $10,000 and $30,000, six states between $30,000 and $50,000, and only one state had more than $50,000. There was a general lack of clinics and public health nurses in rural areas. The depression had a devastating effect also on children of pre-school age and the adolescent group, for inadequate family income meant more malnutrition and an increased number of physical defects which were not corrected. Though private agencies and state departments through programs of preventive medicine had done good work, this was not enough to prevent harmful results to many children. Under Title V of the Social Security Act as revised in 1939, $5,820,000 is appropriated annually for maternal and child health services and allotted to the states by the Children's Bureau. Each state, irrespective of size, receives $20,000, and the remainder is apportioned annually according to the ratio of live births in the state to the total number of live births in the United States, or as the Secretary of Labor feels necessary according to the financial needs of each state. The Children's Bureau must approve the plan, which must provide for financial participation by the state and for administration or supervision by a state health agency.

As recommended, the entire program is to consist of five major services, which are:

1. Prenatal, infant, and pre-school service which shall reach out into rural areas.

2. School health service, including physical and dental examinations at stated intervals and a program of health education.

3. Health service to children entering employment, carried on in coöperation with health agencies in the community.

4. Health service to special groups of children, such as handicapped children, those in institutions, and in families who are on relief; this to be carried on in coöperation with the social service agencies in the community.

5. Public health nursing service for mothers and children, primarily on educational demonstration lines, to include home visits in connection with the maternal and child health program; prenatal and child health conferences, and conferences with the parents in order to bring about correction of defects found in physical examinations. This program is intended to bring about coöperation between individuals and agencies concerned with welfare, education, and health.

Much flexibility has been allowed in working out the plans, that they may be modified from time to time as need arises.

Crippled Children.—Probably more interest has been shown in the care and treatment of crippled children than of any other group, for there is something about their particular handicap that stirs the emotions as nothing else does. For that reason private organizations and many different service groups have for a long time been working in the interests of crippled children. Special hospitals have been established in various parts of the country under the auspices of the Shriners, and many other hospitals have been devoted wholly or partially to crippled children. These private organizations have been pioneers in the work, but it is now partly a matter of governmental concern. Under the Social Security Act, beginning in 1940, $3,870,000 is apportioned annually for crippled children in rural areas and in regions suffering from severe economic distress. Each state receives $20,000, and the remainder is apportioned on the basis of need. The states must match the funds and must use the same for locating crippled children and for providing medical, surgical, and corrective care, as well as facilities for hospitalization and after-care of children who are crippled and for those suffering from conditions which lead to crippling. These services include clinics and follow-up work of the most expert sort, and there is great variation in the plans of the several states.

Two problems are involved in the provisions for crippled children. First, treatment must be given early in the hope that the child can be restored to nearly normal physical condition; and second, when return to normalcy is impossible, training must be available in order that the child can become an asset instead of a liability to society. This involves after-care and education that will bring about a social adjustment, and may mean either placement outside of the child's own home or special teaching in the home. It should most certainly include a social investigation by one who can understand the crippled child and the personality problems which may develop as a result of being different from other children. Sometimes the work is entirely carried on by a state department of health, and in other states it is done by a coöperative service with the different departments of the state or private agencies providing the medical, social, and educational services that are needed.[6]

Child Welfare Services.— Child welfare services, third of the legislative measures designed to promote security for children, is carried on jointly by the state public welfare agency and the Children's Bureau, "for the purpose of establishing, extending, and strengthening, especially in predominately rural areas, public welfare services for the protection and care of homeless, dependent, and neglected children and children in danger of becoming delinquent." One-and-a-half million dollars is appropriated annually for this program, and unlike the funds appropriated for child health services and services for crippled children does not have to be on a matching basis. Every state receives a minimum of $10,000 annually and the remainder is apportioned by the Secretary of Labor on the basis of the ratio of the rural population of the state to the rural population of the country as a whole. The plan submitted by each state must be approved by the Children's Bureau, and while the states do

[6] It should be noted that some states include in the category of crippled children those who have heart trouble, a cleft palate, or harelip. The Children's Bureau accepts the state's definition in working out the program.

not have to match the funds, it is intended that states or local communities shall participate in the financial expenditures and that the responsibility of developing adequate methods of community child welfare organization shall be borne by the local communities. The services are along lines not already covered, and therefore the plans of the several states have been developed to meet local needs instead of conforming to any specific pattern.

It is recognized that children in rural areas need the same protection and care that is available for children in urban areas and many services are given under the program, including:

1. Protection and care of dependent and neglected children who are without proper parental care and guardianship or who are suffering because of the depravity or cruelty of the parents, court action being taken when necessary either to protect the child or prosecute the offender.

2. Placement in foster homes, either boarding homes, free homes, adoption homes, or work or wage homes, depending upon the needs of the child.

3. Careful investigation of all homes offering to care for children or young people.

4. Placement in an institution when a foster home is not suitable, and commitment to an institution through the court when necessary.

5. Preventive work with pre-delinquents.

6. Study of the delinquent and the causes which contribute to the delinquencies, with psychological and psychiatric service as a part of the program.

7. Investigation for courts having to do with children's cases and acting as probation officer if requested.

8. Placement of the mentally defective child in an in-

stitution when necessary or provision for special care and training in the community.

9. Coöperative planning for crippled children by state or private agencies concerned with their welfare.

10. Treatment and education of blind and deaf children.

11. Aid to unmarried mothers through court action, and planning for maternity care and after-care for mother and child.

12. Protection of the illegitimate child, including placement with the mother or in a foster home, or for adoption.

Not all states provide all these services under the child welfare program, because the needs are sometimes met in other ways; but, as can be seen, the concept and interpretation of child welfare is broad, and the preservation of the family unit is emphasized in administering this Act.

Aid to the Needy Blind.— Aid to the needy blind is administered by the Security Board, grants being made to the states as in old age assistance. Twenty-six states had laws providing for allowances to the blind when the Social Security Act was passed, but Massachusetts and Connecticut were the only ones having provisions which enabled them to qualify for federal aid at once.

The Act provides for administration by a state agency, financial participation by the state, and application of the program to all parts of the state. No one is eligible for aid if living in an almshouse, and no person can receive more than $20 a month from a federal grant or both old age assistance and aid to the blind. As 40 per cent of the blind are over sixty-five, this is much the same group who are eligible for old age assistance. As there is no federal age requirement the state laws prescribe the minimum age, which varies from sixteen to sixty, though in most states it is eighteen or twenty-one. The states decide who may receive the grants, but if federal funds are used no state can require more than five years' residence in the state during the preceding nine years or more than one year of continuous residence immediately before the application. In many states a large number of those receiving aid to the blind were formerly the recipients of some form of poor relief. Now, instead of being cared for in almshouses or institutions for paupers, they have their board paid in the homes of friends who look after their interests. In this type of service, too, the social worker helps to budget the needs. Many individuals are placed in employment after a period of training. Three million dollars was appropriated the first fiscal year ending June 30, 1936, and the Act states "an annual amount thereafter sufficient to carry out the purposes of the Act shall be appropriated."

Vocational Rehabilitation.— The Federal Act authorized the appropriation of $1,938,000 after 1937, and in 1939 this was nearly doubled by an added appropriation of $1,562,000. This is allotted to the states on the basis of population and on condition that the states match the amount of the federal funds. The United States Office of Education is given the responsibility in coöperation with the Departments of Education of the several states, for the "vocational rehabilitation of persons who by reason of a physical defect or infirmity, whether congenital or acquired by accident, injury or disease, are incapacitated for remunerative occupation." This is closely allied to the program for crippled children and the services to the blind and deaf, for individuals in these groups are included if they are vocationally handicapped. When this is extended to include those with heart disturbances, as it may be, the assistance may consist of training in a business school or something of that nature. The expense of maintenance cannot be paid from the federal-state funds, however, and private agencies have to help out with maintenance expenses and often with medical treatment. Both are essential and because of a financial deficiency this service is not completely carried on by the joint public funds. Placement is a part of the vocational rehabilitation service and is brought about through the state public employment bureau.

FURTHER HEALTH SERVICES

In addition to the appropriation for maternal and child health service, there is another provision in the Act having to do with the important question of the health of millions of families and individuals who, because of illness, may become beset with fear and insecurity. Since 1799 the federal public health service has been working to control epidemics, establish quarantine regulations, and collect data in order to prevent the introduction and spread of contagious diseases. By 1912 the powers had been broadened by legislative acts to include laboratory stations where scientific methods of disease prevention had been studied. The Security Act by the latest revision provides for an appropriation of $11,000,000 annually for the purpose of assisting the states and political subdivisions in establishing and maintaining adequate public health services. The funds are apportioned to the states by the Surgeon-General of the Public Health Service, with the approval of the Secretary of the Treasury, and are on the basis of population, special health problems, and the financial needs of the states. Funds may be used to assist governmental units in their health programs and also to train nurses and other public health workers. An additional $2,000,000 is appropriated for the investigation of disease, problems of sanitation, and administrative expenses.

Through federal and state participation this entire Social Security program exemplifies the term *coöperation* to an unusual degree, through its attack upon forces that tear down and devastate the lives of human beings. Each division of the Act presents social problems affecting individuals as they live and work, and behind all of these problems there is a background of historical information which could only be touched upon briefly in relation to the Security Act.

11.

A HOME FOR THE FAMILY

THE old saying, a man's home is his castle, is full of meaning and emotional tone because of the memories and experiences that make up family life and the friendships which center about the home. Whether an individual owns his home or lives in one which is owned by another there is a feeling of possession about it. Because millions do live in homes which are owned by others the subject of landlord and tenant, including their rights and duties toward each other, is very important to the family.

A CONTRACTUAL RELATIONSHIP

This relationship is usually entered into by contract, which is either express or implied. By means of the contract the person owning the property, called the landlord or lessor, grants to the tenant, or lessee, the right to use certain property. This may be a house, an apartment, one room, an office, or some interest in land which does not particularly affect the family life, such as a mining or oil-well lease. As this is a contractual relationship it is necessary to conform to the essentials of a legal contract. There must be an agreement by competent parties; property, which is the object of the agreement; and sufficient consideration, which in this type of contract is the rent. There must be delivery and acceptance; usually the contract must be in writing and sometimes under seal.

QUESTIONS WHICH MAY ARISE UNDER THIS RELATIONSHIP

Both the landlord and the tenant need to know about their rights and responsibilities for repairs; the payment of rent; and the assignment or sublease of the property. Among the questions that most often arise are the following: What is the best form of lease, and how long will the lease run if the date is not expressly stipulated? What will happen if the tenant moves out before the expiration of the lease or the property is destroyed? What will constitute an eviction, and how will the lease be terminated? Who is responsible for injuries to the tenant or to a third party if the premises are defective? Who is entitled to improvements made on the property? Both landlord and tenant should be informed on these points.

THE LEASE

A lease is a conveyance of a particular estate in lands, and it conveys less than the entire interest of the lessor. It takes effect only from the time of its delivery and not from the time it is dated, unless otherwise stated, and there can be no delivery without an express or implied acceptance. Delivery implies a manual transfer of possession from one person to another, but entering into possession is sufficient delivery. In a recent case the owner of a piece of land leased it to a tenant who agreed to pay the taxes instead of the rent, as consideration. He did not do this, so after a few years the property was sold to the county for taxes and a tax deed was issued. The tenant then purchased the land from the county and took the title without notice to the former owner. The tenant was guilty of bad faith, for he had written a letter to the landlord in which he recognized him as the owner of the land. When his offer to pay the taxes for the use of the land was accepted and he went into possession, a landlord-tenant relationship was established.[1]

The lease may be either for a fixed term, such as for years, for a week, or for a month; or at the will of the parties, and in the latter case it can be terminated when either party wishes. A lease to a person during minority is a good lease, for the time of attaining majority is definitely fixed by law. A lease may contain an option which gives the lessor or lessee the privilege of continuing the tenancy for a longer period, but the tenancy terminates with the expiration of the term as first agreed unless the option is exercised.

It is said that an oral, or parol lease as it is called, is a very one-sided agreement for it usually benefits the landlord. At common law the tenant was likely to be in an extremely unfair situation and have to pay rent on property after it had been destroyed, or do something else equally inequitable. The subject of leases is now largely controlled by the statutes of the individual states. At common law it was not necessary to have a lease in writ-

---

[1] Wood v. Homelvig, Supreme Court of North Dakota, 283 N. W. 279.

ing regardless of the length of time that it was to run, but in 1677 the very important law previously mentioned, called the Statute of Frauds, was enacted. It was declared that every lease for more than three years should be in writing and signed by the parties, or it would have the effect of a lease at will only. As this statute had not been enacted at the time this country was settled, it did not form a part of the common law which was taken over at that time; but there are now statutes in practically all states based on the Statute of Frauds. Many states require all leases for more than one year to be in writing, though usually it is not necessary to have a seal.

What will constitute sufficient writing has been a fine point of interpretation at times; however, a letter showing a specific offer and one of acceptance is sufficient to constitute a valid lease, but if new terms are proposed in the letter of acceptance no lease exists until the new terms are accepted by the other party. In a very early Massachusetts case a signed and dated receipt on a bill of sale of hay and oats with the memorandum: "Left at stable on O Street where P. takes possession. Rent to begin October 1, 1870, for 1 year at $150."—was held to be a lease, and oral evidence was admitted to show that the premises consisted of a lot of land on which there was a stable.[2]

A lease is construed according to the will of the parties, but an agreement entered into verbally will not hold against the agreement in the lease, though the written portions of a lease hold over the printed ones. The lease must contain a description of the property, and also the restrictions and covenants stating the terms which are binding on the parties. A refusal of either party to take

[2] Eastman v. Perkins, 111 Mass. 30.

or give the lease is a breach of contract and suit may be brought for damages, but first there must be a demand upon the party who is either to give or accept the lease.

If a man leases property which he afterward sells, two situations may arise, depending upon whether there is an oral lease at the will of the parties or a lease in writing. In the first case the tenant is at the mercy of the new owner and has no rights which he can enforce. If there is a written lease the new owner has the right of possession of the property but takes it subject to the lease. Either party may have a right of action if they cannot settle their controversy satisfactorily; the owner might have to evict the tenant if he wished the property, and the tenant on the other hand could sue for damage on account of the loss and inconvenience which it caused him. A great deal depends upon the custom and statutes in the different states.

There is a distinction between a lease and an agreement for a lease. The difference is important, for if it is a present lease it cannot be varied by other evidence and the parties are bound by it. But if it is an agreement for a future lease it is incomplete and may be changed. The intent of the parties which is shown by the terms of the agreement is the test. For example, when A wrote B that he would take a house at a specific rent for two years if the house was painted and B replied that he would accept this offer and immediately painted the house, this was a lease, not an offer of one, for there was nothing left to be completed.

In the main the same parties who are competent to make a valid contract can also make a lease. A lease made by a person *non compos mentis* is void unless it has been executed; one made by a minor is not void but may be avoided. A guardian may lease his minor ward's land during minority, though a single member of a partnership cannot make a valid lease of partnership land.

Usual Covenants.— There is no limit to the number of covenants or agreements which may be inserted in a lease, for the parties can impose liabilities and raise limitations as they wish. The usual ones that are implied, if not expressed, arise by law through the use of certain words, as "grant," "demise," or "lease," and depend upon the practice in the particular community. The most common covenants are that the lessee shall pay rent, keep the premises in repair, and shall have exclusive possession, or right to quiet enjoyment of the property by reason of his interest in it; the landlord shall pay the taxes and have a right to inspect the premises to see that they are kept in good condition. The less usual covenants are that the tenant shall build in case of accidental destruction, shall neither assign, sublease, nor conduct a particular business. Sometimes the rent ceases in case the property is destroyed, and sometimes the landlord has the right of entry if the rent is not paid or if the tenant breaks other agreements.

More About Covenants.— Certain covenants are said to run with the land and to bind not only the tenant who enters under the lease but anyone who may receive the lease from him through assignment or sublease. In an assignment the tenant transfers the whole or part of his interest for the whole period of time, while in a sublease he transfers the whole or part of his interest for a portion of the period only; this creates a new relation of landlord and tenant. It has been held that if an instrument disposes of a whole unexpired term but contains a covenant to surrender the premises on the last day of the term, it is a sublease and not an assignment. A tenant can assign when there is a condition in the lease against subleasing, and, likewise, if there is a condition which prohibits assigning he can sublease without violating the condition. In a few states there are statutes forbidding the transfer of property to another without the consent of the landlord, but in the absence of such a provision in the lease the tenant may assign, sublease, or mortgage the property. A sublease does not affect the liability between the lessor and the lessee, except that the lessee's rights of possession have been transferred to the sub-tenant. There is no contract between the lessor and the sub-tenant and so he is not liable to the original landlord but holds of the lessee, who has become his landlord. The sub-tenant, however, takes the property subject to all the restrictions under which the tenant held it, and if he commits any act which is forbidden this will constitute a breach of condition for which the landlord can enter and terminate the lease. The decisions concerning the responsibility of a sublessee or assignee to build or to make repairs are somewhat in conflict. An old English case held that an agreement to build a wall on a certain part of the property did not bind the sublessee to do this unless the wall was in existence at the time of leasing; an agreement relating to something to be built afterward was not binding.[8] This rule has been followed in many decisions since, but other courts have held that there is no difference between a covenant to improve land by building on it and a covenant to improve the same land by repairing the building already on it.

---

[8] Spencer's case, 5 Coke 16 a.

NO IMPLIED WARRANTY OF FITNESS

Usually there is no implied warranty that a house which is leased is fit for habitation or that the premises are fit for the purposes for which they are hired. The lessee has an opportunity to inspect the premises, and so no duty rests upon the landlord to see that the premises are fit for the use intended by the lessee. Some courts hold contrary to this and if a landlord definitely states that the premises are in good condition when they are not, and prevents the tenant from discovering the defects, he acts fraudulently and the tenant can abandon the lease or sue for damages. However, mere omission to disclose a defect is not fraud. Several states have statutes providing that the lessor of any buildings designed for the residence of human beings must put them in condition fit for occupancy and repair all subsequent dilapidation not due to the tenant's negligence.[4] If this is not done within a reasonable time the tenant may repair and deduct from the rent or vacate and be discharged from the rent entirely. As a general rule the landlord is not responsible for repairs which the tenant makes, as it is a presumption that they are made for the tenant's benefit. If the repairs are fixtures, that is, improvements which are chattels that are annexed to the property so that they become a part of it—as mantels, heaters, and certain plumbing fixtures have sometimes been held to be—a difficult and complicated question may arise. Some courts hold that they may be removed if this can be done without injury

[4] Statutes in California, Montana, Oklahoma, North Dakota, South Dakota.

to the property, while others hold that as they are a part of the realty they cannot be removed without the consent of the owner.

DUTY TOWARD EACH OTHER

During the term of tenancy it is the general rule in the absence of statute, or a contract to repair, or warranty of condition, that the landlord and tenant must use reasonable diligence and care in knowing conditions and in exposing others to danger. Therefore, as a usual thing unless the landlord expressly agrees to make repairs, he is not liable for them or for injuries to third parties because of failure to make them. But this rule is limited and depends upon who has control of the premises, that is, whether the tenant is in sole possession or the landlord retains possession and control, as sometimes happens in the case of halls and stairways. The landlord has then been held responsible, as he is bound to see that stairways and passageways are reasonably safe.[5] A recent case involved a similar situation. A suit was brought by lessee to recover damages sustained as a result of the unlawful invasion of leased premises. The facts were that she had occupied the premises for six years under a verbal lease and when the defendant agreed in writing with the owner to buy the property and employed a contractor to make repairs she was informed that it would be necessary for her to move while the work was being done. She stayed on as she did not wish to move, and led the defendant to believe that she would be willing to submit to the inconvenience of having the remodelling done while in possession of the property. She afterwards claimed that,

[5] Cases in California and New York hold an opposite view.

entirely without her consent, workmen entered and disconnected a water heater. This was in the state of Louisiana and according to the code of that state if workmen who were employed by the landlord entered without a tenant's consent the landlord was liable for all damages, but if the tenant expressly or tacitly consented and permitted workmen to make alterations during the existence of the lease the landlord was not responsible for damage suffered as a consequence. By asking permission to remain she consented and could not recover.[6]

PAYMENT OF RENT

There are several important conditions relating to the payment of rent which need to be understood by those entering into a landlord-tenant agreement. At common law under the feudal system rent was payable in various kinds of services or crops; money was not necessarily an incident as it usually is today. The delivery of the lease is the consideration for the rent, and it is no defense to an action for rent by the landlord that the tenant did not take possession unless the failure was due to the landlord's omission to put the premises in condition as agreed. A landlord is entitled to rent past due, but after the property is sold he cannot claim the proportionate part due him up to the time of sale unless this is provided by statute. Many states now provide for this. The rent is due at the end of the term, whether for a year, quarter, month, or other period, unless otherwise stated; the tenant has the whole of the last day on which to make payment and if he is ejected before that time he may defend an action to collect rent. If the landlord enters except to

[6] Cross v. Breland, La. Ct. of Appeals, 185 So. 542.

demand rent, inspect the property, or make repairs as the lease permits, the tenant may abandon the lease and is released from all liability for further rent; if the landlord does anything which can be construed as an eviction, liability for future rent ceases.

EVICTION

Eviction, which is one way of terminating the lease, is either actual, which occurs when the landlord forcibly ousts the tenant from possession, or constructive, which occurs when the landlord does something which lessens the value of the property to the tenant or renders the enjoyment of the premises impossible; for instance, if he allows a nuisance to be carried on in an adjacent part of the property, or if he leases the premises for a certain purpose and they prove to be unsuitable for the purpose. When a landlord entered on his property and partially destroyed a summer home, he evicted the tenant. Likewise, when a landlord let some strenuous animals onto grounds which were rented for exhibition purposes and the animals dug it up and rendered it unfit for use, this was an eviction. Whether a particular act will amount to an eviction or not is a question of fact and is proved as any other question of fact which is disputed in court.

The courts will enforce a lease if possible, but will nevertheless protect the interests of the tenant, particularly against a sudden ending of the lease. It has therefore become the practice to require a notice to quit before the tenant can be actually expelled. This is usually regulated by statute, and unless a definite time is fixed the time of notice must equal the interval of time between the rent periods, as quarter, month, or week. Death, of course, terminates the lease.

ACTION FOR DISTRESS

The landlord at common law could bring an action to recover the rent, called an action for distress, if rent was in arrears beyond the time allowed by law for payment. By means of this action he could seize the tenant's goods and, as the levy was on the leased premises, he could levy on goods belonging to third parties also. In many states distress is no longer possible, but a process for recovering rent is substituted. In states which do permit the action for distress the landlord can levy on the goods of the tenant only. In several states there is a provision for an attachment in favor of the landlord for the recovery of rent which is different from an attachment which any creditor can bring. It is limited to property which is subject to the landlord's lien, and is controlled by statutes and by the terms of the lease. Before signing a lease a prospective tenant should read it very carefully and if he does not thoroughly understand all the conditions he should consult someone who is familiar with the statutes.

THE GOVERNMENT PLANS FOR HOUSING

Closely allied with the subject of landlord and tenant is the program carried on by the federal government which aims to bring about better housing for tenants and home owners. Through the Home Owners Loan Corporation a person who buys property can receive a loan from the federal government up to 90 per cent of the valuation of the property; he can then pay the loan by monthly installments which are applied on the interest and principal of the loan and the taxes on the property. Therefore, on property worth $10,000 a buyer can make an initial payment of $1,000 and get a loan of $9,000. By this plan the borrower knows exactly the amount which he must pay monthly and the date when the entire loan will be paid, for it is all carefully worked out. Many who usually pay rent have become home owners. Aside from the down payment it is like renting a home, except that at the end of seventeen or twenty years the individual will own his home and during that time will have paid five or five-and-one-half per cent interest. The Government holds the mortgage and the Federal bank that is carrying the loan pays the taxes. According to some officials in this service, there is difficulty if the buyer loses his job or for any other reason is unable to pay. In the District of Columbia it is possible to foreclose in three weeks, but in other states a buyer has been able to escape eviction for a year and make no payments during that time; sometimes it even takes two years to evict an owner. Therefore, the banks which approach this proposition from a business standpoint have not shown much interest in the 90 per cent loan as they have to make the foreclosure and turn the property over to the Federal Housing Association with the buyer already evicted. In the past the laws of many states have aided the small farmers and honest men, who have been trying to buy their homes, by discouraging foreclosure, so these laws which are now in operation are inadequate in the present situation.

12.

CRIMINAL LAW

INDIVIDUAL members of the family sometimes indulge in behavior that is in conflict with the rules of living which well-ordered society prescribes, and through failure to conform to these standards they come in contact with the rigid regulations of the criminal law. This type of behavior is very costly and destructive in its effect, both upon the individual and upon society. Scientific studies and research programs have shown that the causes of criminal behavior are as varied as the individuals concerned; for mental and social unintelligence, hereditary instability, economic dependence, and unwholesome environmental factors, including broken homes, all have their place in the evaluation. It is only through a knowledge of the individual's physical, mental, and emotional make-up and the reaction to environment and the pressure of life that the results, namely, the behavior, can be understood. This is the function of the social forces in the community and not in a strict sense of the criminal law. Through child welfare agencies, character building agencies, church organizations, and school departments we have proof of the psychological truism that habits, either good or bad, formed in childhood are carried over and become a part of adult life. It is evident that the social aspects of the problems of human behavior are allied with preventive measures and that prevention should begin in childhood. Many individuals can be kept from careers of crime by proper training and treatment in their early years.[1]

THE ACT AND THE INDIVIDUAL

From a legal viewpoint criminal law, as one branch of the whole field of law, deals with crimes and punishment and it has seemed more concerned with the act than with the individual or with the causes which contribute to criminal behavior. It is exact in its definitions and uniform in the punishments which are imposed through the courts. For this reason medicine, psychiatry, and social work have not had the recognition by the courts which these sciences should have received, except in the juvenile court where the services have been used and their value understood.

WHAT IS A CRIME?

A crime is a wrongful act, but an act may be wrongful and still not be a crime; for instance, it is ethically wrong to lie about a neighbor but this is not a crime in the legal sense. According to Blackstone, a crime is an act committed or omitted in violation of the public law, either forbidding or commanding it. It is therefore an act which

---

[1] The Harvard Crime Survey carried on by Sheldon and Eleanor Glueck showed that more than nine-tenths of the thousand delinquents studied came from broken or poorly supervised homes; that the same proportion employed their leisure time harmfully, and three-fourths of them had never belonged to supervised clubs or attended vocational classes.

is recognized as being against the welfare of society and is so serious that the state will take action and see that the offender is punished. The acts which are crimes are determined by the statutes of the various states, which have modified and added to the English common law of crimes as it existed when this country was settled. Because the statutes are not uniform an act which is a crime in one state may not be so in another, also an act that was considered a crime in one period of progress may not be considered so at another time. Likewise, the punishment for certain crimes has changed. The ducking stool and the pillory were used in England, but the Quakers very early frowned upon these modes of punishment and they never became a part of the law in Pennsylvania.

A wrongful act may be a tort as well as a crime and so give rise to two rights of action, one civil and the other criminal. As an example, if a man quarrels with another man and knocks him down, this is a crime which is against the peace and security of the public, and the state will prosecute for assault and battery; but the injured person has a right to bring an action for damages, also. As both actions can be maintained, bringing one does not bar the other. There are many other instances where dual rights exist, as in larceny, robbery, or failure of duty amounting to negligence, which are all crimes but cause damage and loss to the individual as well.

THREE CLASSES OF CRIMES

Treason.— Crimes are classified as treasons, felonies, and misdemeanors. At common law high treason consisted of causing the death of the sovereign, levying war, or certain other acts against the sovereign. Petit treason at common law arose when a superior was killed by an inferior, as for instance a husband by his wife or a master by his servant. The act that was petit treason at common law is a felony in this country and may be murder or manslaughter, according to the circumstances. The Constitution states: "Treason against the United States consists only in levying war against them, or in adhering to their enemies, giving them aid and comfort." There may also be treason against the individual state, and in either case it is considered the greatest of all crimes because it seeks to undermine the very existence of the government and to overthrow it or betray it to the enemy.

Felony.— A felony at common law included all the other crimes except treason which were punishable by the forfeiture of property and usually by death also. In this country a felony is usually held to be any offense which may be punished by death or confinement in a state prison, and because of our more complex mode of living many social, industrial, and commercial offenses are included that were unknown at common law. There are now only a few crimes which carry the death penalty.

Misdemeanor.— Misdemeanors include all crimes which are less than felonies, and are punishable by a fine or jail sentence.

TYPES OF CRIMES

A further classification of crimes divides them into crimes against the state or public administration and those against the public peace; crimes against public morals, such as seduction and various sex crimes; those against the person, including murder, manslaughter, assault and battery, and kidnapping; and, finally, those against real or personal property.

THE ELEMENTS OF A CRIME

Every crime consists of two elements, the criminal act or omission and the intent. The intent is presumed from the act when any person, except one whose mind is not capable of entertaining intent, commits an act which is prohibited by law. The act and intent must both exist, and mere intent to do an act which would be a crime is not a crime, though it may be an attempt. If a man walks along the street intending to pick another's pocket and actually puts his hand in the other man's pocket but takes nothing because there is nothing in the pocket, that is not larceny but an attempt at larceny. Likewise, if a man intends to take a coat belonging to another and actually takes the coat and then finds it is his own coat, there is no larceny. The intent must not be confused with the motive, for the latter is the reason for doing the act while the intent is the determination to do it.

The motive may be good but if the act is prohibited by law it is a crime, as for example the practice of polygamy on the grounds of religious belief. A man was indicted for bigamy and said he was a Mormon and that as a part of his religious belief he could marry as many women as he could support. This was held to be no excuse.[2]

It is an established rule of criminal law that everyone is liable not only for an act which he actually intends and commits, but for all the natural and direct consequences of the act; so if a man enters a house intending to commit a burglary and while there kills the owner of the home,

[2] Reynolds v. U. S., 98 U. S. 145.

he is guilty of the latter crime for it is presumed that he intends the consequences resulting from his act. These were the exact facts in a New Hampshire case, and when the man was killed it was held to be murder in the first degree, though not committed with a deliberate and premeditated design to kill.[8] This is called constructive intent. The mental elements which constitute criminal intent differ in the various crimes and are expressed by specific words in some instances; for example, in murder it is necessary to have malice aforethought, in larceny there must be a felonious taking and carrying away of the goods of another, and in embezzlement, which was not an offense at common law, the intent to defraud is a necessary element.

No person can be guilty of a crime unless he has sufficient mental capacity to entertain the necessary intent, and the law makes certain exceptions with this in mind. At common law a child under seven was presumed incapable of entertaining criminal intent, between seven and fourteen the usual presumption was that the infant lacked discretion or criminal capacity, but over fourteen he was presumed to have sufficient capacity and this had to be met by counter proof. A person so insane that he is incapable of distinguishing right from wrong is unable to have criminal intent and is hence incapable of committing a crime. No person can be tried, sentenced, or punished for a crime while insane. Some courts recognize irresistible impulse as a good defense, and if the act is the result of such an impulse there is no responsibility. But on this point one court has said that not every slight aberration or derangement will excuse violation of

---

[8] State v. Pike, 49 N. H. 400.

the law.[4] There is criminal responsibility if there is mental capacity sufficient to fully comprehend the nature and consequences of the act. If a man is so drunk that he does not know what he was doing, he may be incapable of entertaining the intent necessary, though usually it is held that voluntary intoxication is no excuse for the commission of the act. It is admissible as evidence to determine the degree of the crime in some instances, and proof of it may reduce murder to manslaughter.

ACTS LEGAL IF COMMITTED BY AN OFFICER

An act which would be a crime if committed by an ordinary individual is excused if committed by an officer in the performance of his duty; hence, when an officer shoots to prevent a prisoner from escaping and the person is killed by the shot this is not homicide. At common law this privilege of shooting to prevent the escape of a prisoner extended to anyone who saw a felony committed; but at the present time no one but an officer of the law is justified in killing another to prevent a felony. It is recognized, however, that anyone may go this far in self-defense if, without fault on his part, he is attacked by another who indicates that he intends to kill and gives reason to believe that he will be able to carry out this intent. Along with this goes the very old rule that one must "retreat to the wall" if by so doing he can avoid the actual use of force. In a certain case a son shot his father with a gun, causing such a serious wound that he died shortly afterward. The evidence showed that the father had become very angry with his son and at the

---

[4] Swaine v. State, Supreme Court of Indiana, 18 N. E. 2nd Series 937.

time the shot was fired was pursuing him with a pitchfork. The jury had to decide whether on the facts they might conclude that the father intended to take the life of his son, or, on the other hand, they might believe that the son could have protected himself by retreating. The rule followed was that when it is possible to retreat one is not justified in taking the life of another.[5]

Defense of one's family stands on the same footing before the law as self-defense, but one can use only reasonable force to defend property and this must not endanger life. Certain acts of defense are allowed, however, if one is attacked and retreats to one's home, for then he need not retreat farther than the threshold.

Ignorance or mistake concerning the facts may be a good defense to a crime, so if a person acts on a bona fide but untrue belief as to the facts he is held responsible only for the act which he thought he was committing. In an old English case a man killed another, thinking he was killing a burglar in his house when actually it was his servant whom he killed. This was called neither murder nor manslaughter but misadventure. However, ignorance of the law is no defense. It is said that this is a rule of necessity for if one could allege ignorance of the law to excuse a criminal act it would never be possible to convict anyone.

PARTIES TO A CRIME

The parties who participate in any crime which is serious enough to be a felony are principals and accessories. At common law this classification was according to the nearness or remoteness of their connection with

---

[5] State v. Donnelly, 69 Iowa 705.

the crime. The principal actually commits the crime, and at common law and in some states there is a distinction between principal in the first and second degree—the latter being one who does not actually commit the crime but who is present at the time and gives aid and encouragement. In misdemeanors all are principals. Accessories assist in a variety of ways, which may be either before or after the crime. The accessory before the fact is one who is not present at the actual commission of the crime but procures or advises another to commit it, while the accessory after the fact receives, comforts, or assists the principal to avoid punishment by helping him to escape, by concealing him, or by suppressing testimony against him. At common law the wife's duty to aid and succor her husband prevented her from being an accessory after the fact.

JURISDICTION OF THE CRIME

Jurisdiction includes the power to hear the facts and determine the crime. The place where the crime takes effect is the locality of the crime; and so if a man stands in one state and intentionally fires a gun at another person across the line in an adjoining state and injures him, it has been held that the state which is the domicile of the injured party has jurisdiction for punishing the offender.[6] Contrary to this rule, one court has held that when cattle were stolen in one county and brought into another county the offender could be tried for larceny in the county into which the stolen property was taken.[7] This is on the theory that it is a continuing crime and there is

[6] Commonwealth v. Macloon, 101 Mass. 1.

[7] State v. Bockman, Supreme Court of Missouri, 1939.

a new taking and larceny in every jurisdiction into which the property is brought. As a rule the jurisdiction of a county extends only to its boundaries unless it is bounded by the high seas, in which case the government has a quasi territorial jurisdiction for three miles out to sea.

EXTRADITION PROCESS

If the guilty person escapes into another state after committing a crime, he is a fugitive from justice. He cannot be punished where he is found for he has committed no crime there, and an officer from the state in which he has committed the crime cannot go into another state to arrest him. The only way that he can be brought back to the state from which he fled is by the process of extradition, which can rightly be considered as part of criminal law procedure. The Constitution provides that any state of refuge shall surrender a fugitive from another state, and the procedure is by application to the governor of the state of refuge by the governor of the demanding state. This is accompanied by a copy of the indictment found, or complaint made to a magistrate, in the demanding state and certified by the governor as authentic. If the governor of the state of refuge is convinced that the accused is a fugitive from justice he issues a warrant to the agent of the demanding state, who arrests and removes the prisoner. Extradition cannot be denied on the ground that the act which has been committed is not a crime in the state of refuge if it is a crime in the demanding state, and while the governor cannot be compelled to issue a warrant he is expected to do so, for the judicial proceedings of one state have full faith and credit in every other state.[8]

[8] See Constitution of the United States, Article IV, Sec. I.

13.

COURT PROCEDURE

JUST as the principles of criminal law were crystallized through the years, so a criminal procedure was developed which controlled the processes by which one accused of a crime was arrested, tried, and punished if convicted. The criminal procedure of the common law which was in effect in England was the result of many centuries of development on the continent, and was brought to this country by the early settlers. It was very harsh and oppressive and gradually was changed somewhat to meet the customs and usages in a new country; nevertheless the criminal procedure of the common law is still the backbone of our present system.

THE ARREST AND PRELIMINARY HEARING

The first step in the process is usually the arrest of the accused person. A warrant which has been issued by a magistrate upon the sworn statement of the complainant is generally necessary before the arrest. However, an officer or even a private individual may make an arrest if an emergency exists; namely, if a felony has been committed or there is a breach of the peace and the safety of the public is endangered. The warrant may be called an order which allows the arrest, and it must state exactly the nature of the charge and the name and description of the person. This rule is so strictly followed that when a person was arrested upon a warrant charging that he did unlawfully, willfully, and feloniously assault another with a deadly weapon with intent to kill, he could not be tried on a charge of assault with a deadly weapon. The decision was that the court had no power to permit an amendment of the warrant and so change it to charge a different offense.[1] In an early New Hampshire case a writ directed the arrest of one George Melvil but was served on George Melvin. He brought suit for false imprisonment and obtained a verdict in his favor, for it is a well settled rule that anyone who causes another to be arrested by a wrong name is a trespasser, even though the warrant was intended for the person actually arrested.[2]

The law affords protection to all persons, whether guilty or innocent, and concedes the accused the right to a speedy trial. If the crime is a minor offense which is within the jurisdiction of a magistrate or police court judge, the matter can be disposed of quickly and a fine or other punishment meted out; but if the offense is a major crime, as murder or misappropriation of funds, the preliminary hearing determines only the fact of sufficient evidence to prove a *prima facie* case. In the latter event the prisoner must then await further proceedings either in jail or out on bail. If bail is allowed a bond is filed to assure his appearance for further examination, and if he fails to appear as required the money is forfeited. The bond should be sufficient to insure the appearance of the accused in court, and it can readily be seen that it must

[1] State v. Clegg, 214 N. C. 677.
[2] Melvin v. Fisher, 8 N. H. 406.

be large enough so that it will not be less burdensome to escape and forfeit the bail than it is to stand trial. It is also evident that bail cannot be allowed in certain cases where the risk of escape is too great. The individual must then be kept in confinement until trial. The trial is sometimes delayed for several months, depending upon the frequency of the terms of court and the crowded state of the docket.

INDICTMENT BY THE GRAND JURY

Before the actual trial the individual must be formally accused of the crime, usually through indictment by the grand jury. This jury consists of not less than twelve nor more than twenty-three persons who are chosen at large from the county having jurisdiction; Blackstone said some should be picked from every hundred and added, "They are usually gentlemen of the best figure in the country." The jury is impaneled at the opening of the term of court, is given a few instructions by the judge, and then retires to carry on its deliberations. The sessions of the grand jury are private, and no one comes before this body except the witnesses, who usually appear singly, and the prosecuting officer, who is the district attorney, state's attorney, or county solicitor. This official holds a very important position, both before the grand jury and later at the trial, for he is the one who conducts the prosecution in the name of the state or commonwealth. He prepares the case and presents the state's side, examines the witnesses and admits only legal evidence. Though he must not express an opinion or take any part in the discussion in order to influence the jury, he may advise as to the law. At least twelve of the men who make up the grand jury must agree in finding a "true bill," which means that they believe the charges stated in the bill and that there is sufficient evidence against the accused to justify a trial. This is endorsed as a "true bill" and when the jury has finished its work all "true bills" are handed to the foreman of the jury, who files them with the clerk. The bills then become indictments. Though the arrest of the offender usually takes place before the indictment, it is sometimes advisable to secure the indictment first. For instance, if a young girl has been the victim of a sex crime, it is a desirable method of procedure as it eliminates one appearance in court and makes a trying experience a little easier for her.

The time element is also important sometimes, particularly in states which have few trial terms of court, for a case that has been brought to the attention of the prosecuting officer at the last moment can be brought directly before the grand jury, and consideration by the lower court eliminated.

Language of the Indictment.— The indictment must be clear and certain in its language as to the charge against the accused, or respondent as he is called. It must set forth the name exactly so there will be no question as to the identity of the person, and it must state the offense and allege a date. At common law it was not proper to allege "on or about" a certain date though this is permissible now by statutes in many states; for example, the date alleged in a case of rape does not have to be exact, thereby allowing the prosecutor latitude in proving the fact without being bound to prove the exact time. If the date is essential in proving the offense, as it is if liquor has been sold on a holiday when it is forbidden by law, it must be stated exactly. The exact description of the premises is necessary when arson or burglary of a certain place is alleged. This accuracy is to assist the accused in order that he may know what to prepare for a defense, as time or place are often important in proving an alibi. The conclusion of the indictment charges that the offense was against the peace of the state.

THE ARRAIGNMENT AND PLEADING

Up to this point the accused has had a hearing in the lower court and been held for the grand jury, which brought an indictment against him, but there is still a possibility that he is not guilty. The law presumes everyone innocent until proven guilty. At the arraignment, which is the next step, the accused is given an opportunity to say whether he is guilty or not. He is brought into court, the accusation contained in the indictment is read to him, and he is required to answer it by pleading guilty, not guilty, or *nolo contendere*. By means of this last plea he does not admit his guilt directly but tacitly admits it by throwing himself on the mercy of the court. If he answers with a plea of guilty the judge can sentence at once, but if the plea is not guilty an issue is formed, which indicates that a fact is affirmed by one side and denied by the other. The case then goes to trial before the jury.

TRIAL BY JURY

The petit jury before which the case is tried has nothing to do with the grand jury, but hears the evidence presented by both sides and bases a verdict upon this. It is supposed to be an impartial body, and the twelve members of the jury must bring in a unanimous verdict.

NOL PROSSING A CASE

At any time before the trial the prosecuting attorney has the right to *nol pros* a case if in his opinion the state cannot prove the allegations; for example, if the main witness for the state is a feebleminded girl and the attorney feels doubtful of her credibility as a witness. This is usually done only after consulting with the court.

PRESERVING THE RIGHTS OF THE ACCUSED

There are various methods of procedure for preserving the rights of the accused, among them change of *venue*. This is allowed when there is such prejudice against the accused that he cannot secure a fair and impartial trial in the county having jurisdiction. The trial is accordingly transferred to another county. In a recent case before the Supreme Court in Texas a change of *venue* was denied because the application was supported solely by the affidavit of the defendant before his counsel and did not show that he would be denied a fair trial.[8] The accused has a right to be defended, and the state may appoint a lawyer if the accused cannot afford one, though a counsel is not always provided unless the crime is a serious felony.

Attorneys may bring various motions which will delay the case; for example, they can claim irregularities in the grand jury procedure, either that the facts stated in the indictment are untrue, or do not constitute a crime in

---

[8] Herrera v. State, 124 S. W. 2nd 147.

that particular state, or that the court does not have jurisdiction. When all the evidence has been presented, the final steps are the verdict by the jury and the sentence of the court if the accused is found guilty.

SENTENCE

The punishment may be a fine or imprisonment or a suspended sentence; and in some states the death penalty is still in force for certain crimes. It should be understood that the jury does not pass on matters of law, so the sentence is imposed by the judge. The accused is in court and he may state any reason why the sentence should not be imposed; in most criminal cases there may be an appeal from the decision as in a civil case. If the accused has been acquitted or convicted a well known rule, called the plea of former jeopardy, protects him in the future, for no person can be tried twice for the same offense; and so if he has been indicted, tried, and either acquitted or convicted, this may be set up as a defense to prevent further prosecution. What will constitute the same offense is sometimes a matter of doubt, but the test commonly followed is: Could the accused have been convicted on the first indictment by proof of the facts alleged in the second? For instance, a man was indicted for killing another by shooting and was found not guilty. He was then indicted and convicted for killing the same man by striking him with a gun. This conviction was held proper, for the evidence necessary to sustain the second indictment would not have been proper under the first so he was not placed in jeopardy twice for the same offense.[4] It is presumed to be for the interest of so-

[4] Guedel v. People, 43 Ill. 226.

ciety as well as the individual that there should be an end to the controversy. Hence, there are statutes barring a prosecution unless it is started within a prescribed time, which varies according to the offense.

CONDUCTING A CIVIL CASE

The steps in the trial of a civil case are not the same as in a criminal case. The parties to an action of this sort may be individuals or corporations, and the state as an entity is not a party. When one contemplates legal action, he should consult an attorney as to his rights. The attorney will get all the facts which have to do with the case and eliminate those which have no legal significance. For example, in the case of an accident it is important to know who saw it and all the relevant facts to which the law can be applied, such as the time, place, and persons connected with it.

If the plaintiff's attorney decides there is a good case, a notice is served on the defendant, who is the person against whom the claim is brought, to appear in court at a specified time. This brings him under the jurisdiction of the court. At the hearing if no case is established the matter is ended at once; it may also be ended if the suit is for a small amount of damages and is within the jurisdiction of the magistrate or police court. But if the decision is adverse to the defendant he may appeal and this transfers the case to the regular trial court, or it may be started there in the first instance by filing a summons or writ and a statement of claim. The defendant files an answer so that, as in criminal procedure, an issue is formed and it is upon this issue that the trial proceeds, either before a judge or a judge and jury. The facts of the plaintiff's claim are first presented and if a case is made out the defendant proceeds with his answering testimony. The jury determines the facts, the judge applies the law to them, and the verdict, which is called a judgment in a civil suit, is handed down. The execution is the final process unless the losing party takes an appeal from the judgment of the court. This procedure may be somewhat simplified but it is essentially the course of action in following a civil case through the courts.

14.

EVIDENCE

THE rules of law are divided into two classes: those which prescribe the rights and obligations of men and are known as rules of "substantive law," and those which relate to the means of enforcing these rights and obligations and are called rules of "adjective law." The law of evidence belongs in the latter class, as it relates to the use of evidence, the rules for its exclusion and for presenting it in court.

WHAT IS EVIDENCE?

The law of evidence should not be confused with evidence itself. The latter includes all the legal means, exclusive of mere arguments, which tend to prove or disprove any matter of fact that is submitted to judicial investigation.[1] In other words, it is the means by which disputed facts are proven in a court of law. Sometimes testimony is used synonymously with evidence, but actually testimony is only one form of evidence and does not include writings, documents, or real evidence which may be used in the course of a trial to establish proof.

[1] John J. McKelvie, *Handbook of the Law of Evidence*, p. 7.

JUDICIAL NOTICE

As just stated, the facts in issue are established by means of evidence, but there are certain facts which do not have to be proved, because they are so well known, or so easy to ascertain that it would be a waste of time to be obliged to demonstrate their accuracy. Therefore it is a rule that the court will take judicial notice of certain truths, such as facts of governmental concern which relate to national or state government; the jurisdiction and decisions of its own court; the phenomena of nature and the physical sciences that have become such a part of our habits of thought that they are not disputed, such as the nature and effect of heat or cold. Matters relating to customs, habits, and the lives of mankind do not have to be proved if they are facts which are universally recognized, for example, that a telephone will conduct messages from one point to another, or that automobiles have largely replaced horses in our cities. In a case which was decided for the plaintiff and later reversed it was said to be common knowledge that a moving picture theater necessarily operates in partial darkness. The action was for personal injuries that were received when a patron of the theater became dissatisfied with her seat and moved to a place she thought was more desirable. She claimed there was no usher to assist her and that the theater was not properly lighted. She knew she had to go down steps to get to the other part of the theater and admitted that she could not see these at all. On an appeal the decision was against her because she was negligent in moving when she could not see.[2] Facts admitted by the parties

[2] Olsen v. Edgerly, Indiana Court, 18 N. E. 2nd Series 937.

by means of written pleadings require no proof, as they are acknowledged; also any further admissions which are made by either party in open court, in order to expedite the trial when proof would otherwise be needed, are in the same class.

THE BURDEN OF PROOF

Before considering the form and nature of evidence and the facts which will be excluded or admitted we need to understand in some detail the systematic method of presenting evidence and the fact that the person who makes an allegation in the pleading has to prove it. That is, according to legal rule, "the burden of proof" rests on the one who would be defeated if no evidence were given on either side. Long years of usage have established this as a definite rule in trying cases; therefore, if the plaintiff alleges certain facts in the pleading which the defendant denies in the answer, the plaintiff must assume the burden of proof throughout the trial; but the defendant at times may have the burden of going on with evidence to support his denial of the claim made by the other party. The following case will illustrate this: plaintiff alleged that he was owner of certain property, and that in June 1937 he leased the premises, in writing, to the defendant for such time as would be necessary to cultivate and gather a crop of cotton then growing on the premises; that defendant had gathered the crop of cotton on or about the 25th of July 1938 but still held possession of the premises against the will and consent of the plaintiff, though plaintiff had made a written demand for possession. The complaints also alleged that the defendant did not have any lease on the premises nor any right to possession. Defendant answered, admitting plaintiff's ownership of the property, that it was leased as plaintiff alleged and the original lease had expired, but he claimed possession under a new oral lease. The real issue at the trial was whether or not there was a new oral lease, and the jury was instructed that the burden of proof was upon the plaintiff and never shifts, although the burden of procedure may shift, as in this case, when the burden of proving a new lease was on the defendant.[3] The verdict is given according to whether the allegation is sustained or denied, and if the evidence is evenly balanced the verdict must be against the person who has the burden of proof, because he did not establish his allegation by a preponderance of evidence, which is the test in civil cases. In criminal cases the burden of proof is on the state and it must be shown beyond a reasonable doubt that the accused is guilty.

PRESUMPTIONS

There are certain presumptions indirectly connected with the law of evidence which are not substitutes for inference but are definite rules based upon experience or public policy and imposed for the convenience of the jury in order that it may be easier to determine the truth. McKelvey states that these rules have developed through four stages. "The first stage was that of mere inference which was permissible; the second stage was a disposition on the part of the judge to advise the jury as to the desirability of such inference; the third, instruction that

[3] Harvey v. Aubrey, Supreme Court of Arizona.

such an inference ought to be drawn; and, finally, a rule that the inference was a necessary one which the jury was bound to draw." In this way it became equivalent to saying that certain things are true, though any presumption is rebuttable and may be disproved by proper evidence. Some of the best known *prima facie* presumptions are: absence of a person for seven years, without communication with those who would naturally hear from the person if alive, gives rise to a presumption of death; evidence that a child is born during marriage is sufficient to establish the presumption of legitimacy; evidence of mailing a letter is on its face sufficient to prove receipt of the letter.

A case in point concerned two promissory notes payable with interest at six per cent which plaintiff tried to collect from defendant. Three letters were introduced as evidence—one written to defendant on July 27, 1935; a second followed this on August 2 of the same year; the third was an answer from defendant. The first letter was returned because of an incorrect address and was forwarded to the new address. The second letter did not make a demand for the money but asked for a reply to the first letter in which a demand had been made. In reply defendant wrote of his hard luck and inability to pay as agreed but proposed that the payments should be made over a period of time. Plaintiff accepted the proposal. At the time of the trial defendant claimed that he did not receive the first letter though there was no evidence offered to support this. The decision was that his letter was in answer to the first letter, for when plaintiff testified that he wrote and mailed a letter to defendant and there was no evidence that the letter was not received by defendant, the presumption was that the letter was written and properly posted and therefore was received.[4]

CLASSIFICATION OF EVIDENCE

Evidence may be classified as real evidence, written evidence, and testimonial evidence. The last mentioned may be either direct or circumstantial.

Real Evidence.— Real evidence is a tangible or physical object which the jury can see in court, such as a gun that has been used in a murder, or a hand which has been mutilated by an accident. This type of evidence is sometimes called demonstrative evidence. A ruling which permitted the exhibition of an injured shoulder and plaster cast was held not to be an abuse of the trial court's discretionary power, in a personal injury suit.[5] Land may be the subject of the controversy, and sometimes it is necessary for the jury to inspect the property in order to obtain real evidence.

A writing or document when treated as a physical object and examined in court may be regarded as real evidence. If its existence is material to the case, its presentation is proof just as the presentation of any article would be. In a more restricted sense writings are looked upon as the expression of certain operative acts which pass something from one party to another. A will or a deed is an example. Proof of their authenticity and the manner of producing them in court have presented difficulties at times.

Writings.— The contents of a writing must be proved by the introduction of the writing itself if it is in existence,

---

[4] Cady v. Guess, Supreme Court of Arkansas, 124 S. W. 213.

[5] Dinwiddie v. Siefkin, 20 N. C. 2nd Series 130.

as this is the best evidence available; but if the document is lost or destroyed, copies which have been compared with the original are admissible as secondary evidence. When the carbon copy of a written contract, the existence of which was in question, was offered without proper identification as a duplicate of the original, and without adequate explanation of the failure to produce the original, it could not be accepted as evidence.[6] Writings are proved in two ways; attested documents are proved by the attesting witness if alive; unattested documents by evidence that the handwriting of the maker is genuine. Public records and court records can be proved by certified copies, as the originals are not as a rule available for court purposes.

Testimonial Evidence.— Evidence secured by means of witnesses is of great importance and may be either direct or circumstantial. The first is the direct testimony of one who saw or heard certain things which prove the fact in dispute, while indirect or circumstantial evidence establishes a fact from which the fact in dispute is inferred. An example of this is shown in the trial for the theft of an automobile. A has an automobile stolen from his premises and if B can testify that he saw C go into A's garage and drive the car out, that is direct evidence. However, the theft of an automobile is not usually made as boldly as that, so if it can be shown that simultaneously with the loss of the car, C is absent from town, and he is located in a distant city with a car of the same make and number as the stolen car, it can be inferred from all the circumstances that he took it though no one actually saw him do so. It is said that circumstantial evidence is

---

[6] Campbell et al. v. People's Savings Bank & Trust Company, 214 N. C. 680.

not as strong as direct evidence but many times it is the only evidence obtainable.

EVIDENCE OF FORMER ACTS NOT ADMISSIBLE

The same case can be used to illustrate a further rule. It might be helpful in proving this theft to show that C had previously been guilty of appropriating things belonging to others; but this evidence is not admissible, for the law does not allow the inference that a person who has committed a criminal act once is likely to do so again. This might seem to be the logical and relevant inference about a person's character, but the commission of one crime is not admissible to prove another, and character cannot be proved by former acts. When character is an issue it is proved by evidence of the general reputation of the person in the community. As it is necessary to exclude any evidence which might confuse or prejudice the jury, this rule aids the accused and gives him a chance to safeguard his rights.

HEARSAY EVIDENCE

In order to be admissible, evidence must be competent as well as relevant; and when applied to evidence, competency relates to the form of presentation. The general class of evidence which is not admissible because it is incompetent is hearsay evidence; but no sooner does the law of evidence rule that hearsay is inadmissible than it turns about and makes exceptions. As a general rule statements, either oral or written, which are made by persons who are neither parties to the suit nor witnesses, are not admissible. In other words, if a person cannot state of his own knowledge that a fact is true, but only that someone told him so, this is hearsay. The reason for excluding this type of evidence is fairly obvious. When a person is testifying before the court he is under oath to speak the truth and is subject to cross-examination; but this is not the case with hearsay evidence, for the person who made the original statement is not before the court, is not under oath, and his testimony can neither be refuted, explained, nor investigated by cross-examination. To illustrate, A sues B for the price of a watch which he sold B. B offers the testimony of C, who says D examined the watch and said it was not in good condition anyway. This is inadmissible, as D, the person who could give the information, is not before the court. Hearsay is admissible when the circumstances tend to insure the truth of the evidence, or because the declaration of certain parties who cannot be witnesses is the best evidence obtainable.

Confessions and admissions are strictly speaking examples of hearsay which are admissible as evidence, for in both of these statements the person makes an acknowledgement which is against his own interest, and it is not reasonable to suppose he would do this unless the statement were true.

Confessions.— A confession is an acknowledgement by a person that he is guilty of the crime with which he is charged and is therefore admissible only in criminal cases. In addition it must be shown that the confession is offered voluntarily and is not the result of promises of favor or threats and acts of torture, which was the ancient method of exacting confessions. The torture was often so severe that innocent persons, in order to escape it, would confess crimes which they had not committed.

Admissions.— An admission is a statement or act which amounts to an affirmation of some fact which is material to the issue and which operates at the time of trial against the interest of the party making it; it may be used in either criminal or civil cases, though in the former it is not as inclusive as a confession. Various declarations are an exception to the rule against hearsay because they are the best evidence that can be obtained. Some of these are:

1. Declarations against pecuniary or proprietory interest are admissible when made by a party who has since died. An entry in a book which shows the receipt of money is an example of this.
2. Dying declarations are admissible when made in the expectation of death, because it is assumed that under these conditions they will be true.
3. Declarations concerning matters of public interest are allowed as proof; ancient documents and public records are admissible on the theory that they are likely to be correct.
4. Entries in the course of business, which include not only commercial business but professional services as well, are allowed because of the same assumption that they are likely to be correct.
5. Testimony and declarations made under oath may with certain qualifications be presented as evidence when the witness is dead or physically or mentally incapable of being present.
6. Declarations relating to pedigree, and the testimony of a person relative to his own age, though hearsay, are admissible facts because they are based on family tradition.

An interesting example of this rule is the following. By the law of Oregon, property left by an illegitimate child goes to the state if the person dies without a will. In an action brought by the state for the estate of Arthur W. Wakefield valued at $9,000, the following facts were brought out. Two women claimed to be his half-sisters and his sole surviving heirs at law; the state admitted that they had the same mother but claimed there was no proof of a marriage between the mother and father of deceased. Testimony of a half-sister was admitted and she said the parents were married and soon after the marriage the father of the deceased joined the army and was killed. For some reason her mother resumed her maiden name of Wakefield and brought her son up by that name. She later married the father of the two half-sisters who claimed the estate. This evidence was admitted, for a daughter's testimony concerning her deceased mother's statements about the circumstances of her marriage as affecting the legitimacy of her son, is admissible as an exception to the general hearsay rule since it relates to history and family tradition concerning pedigree.[7]

WITNESSES

The judicial inquiry should be as complete as possible; therefore anyone who has knowledge of the matter in controversy can be summoned to appear as a witness and is not excused without good reason. In England the early practice was to exclude many persons from this duty. This was largely a result of the social and political life which fostered inequalities between the sexes, and between those of different religious and political beliefs. Those excluded from testifying were persons who held peculiar religious beliefs or had no religious beliefs, and

[7] *In re* Wakefield Estate, 87 Pacific 2nd Series 794.

so were not bound by an oath; the parties to the suit; a husband or a wife of the parties to the suit; persons who had a pecuniary interest; naturally incapacitated persons; and those guilty of certain crimes. Most of these exclusions have been removed, but under certain circumstances a person may claim privilege and hence is not forced to testify; for example, a person accused of a crime may testify, but if he wishes to refuse he may do so and his refusal cannot be used as the basis of an inference against him. Communications between attorney and client and other similar associations which relate to matters of professional employment are privileged. An attorney is neither compelled nor permitted, without the consent of his client, to disclose communications which have been made to him. Communications between a husband and wife are privileged on the basis of unity of interest and the sanctity of the home. All persons may refuse to testify as to state secrets.

EXPERT OPINION

It is an ancient rule of law that inferences are for the jury and that a witness must testify concerning the facts only, which for the purpose of evidence relate to something capable of being known through the senses, such as sight and hearing. It follows as a general rule that the opinion of a witness is inadmissible, but "expert opinion" constitutes an exception to this rule. Such evidence is admitted only on matters which the jury, being composed of average men without special training, are incapable of judging without assistance. Two questions are involved in determining its admissibility: first, does the subject matter require expert opinion? And secondly, is the person who is offered as a witness an expert on the subject? The first is based on the assistance which the testimony will give to the jury; the second upon the qualifications of the witness, in the field in which he claims to be an authority. While the two best known subjects of opinion evidence are handwriting and sanity, the law recognizes experts in other fields if they are skilled through special study. The testimony of experts is contradicted only by the testimony of other experts and leaves the jury in the position of deciding which to believe. The most usual method of presenting the opinion of expert witnesses is by means of the hypothetical question, which relates to the result that would follow from certain assumed facts. As an example, if a physician is on trial for the negligent treatment of a crippled child, certain symptoms can be enumerated and an orthopedic specialist can be asked what treatment he would give; but the specialist is not allowed to offer his opinion concerning the negligence of the other physician, nor can he be asked for his opinion of the treatment given, according to the evidence which he has heard in court. These are facts on which the jury alone must decide.

LEGAL AND SOCIAL EVIDENCE

Probably most people have less understanding about court procedure and evidence than almost any other division of the legal field, and therefore more readily form unfair conclusions. This is even true to a large extent of the group who are familiar with the methods of gathering, evaluating, and interpreting information in the fields of science, medicine, and social work. The aim of all these groups is service to individuals who need help because of some crisis in their lives; and medicine, social work, and law move toward this end by means of certain processes of research, interpretation, and treatment which differ somewhat in method but are similar in many ways. Medicine and social work base their interpretation upon more flexible data than law, and the decision may be delayed for the factors change from day to day. It is this same flexible quality which makes it difficult for social workers to understand the difference between social and legal evidence.[8] It should be understood that if the latter must be presented in a way which seems rigid and unsocial in its restrictions, it is largely because the customs which developed from crude beginnings have hampered progress and made it hard to break away from tradition; furthermore, if law is necessary in order to control the conduct of individuals in society, the facts reported by means of evidence must be accurate, as they form the basis for a final and permanent conclusion.

---

[8] For a discussion of evidence read Mary E. Richmond, *Social Diagnosis.*

15.

CONCLUSIONS

CERTAIN of the foregoing chapters should have made it evident that there has been marked mutability in many fields of law, particularly in those which relate to women and children. To sum up, we now find more regard for woman as a legal personality than in the past, and a greater parity with man in her responsibility for and control of children and property. Also, we find a deeper concern for all members of society, but particularly for children and those who are unable to care for themselves. This is shown in the juvenile court laws and the social security legislation.

THE FORCES WHICH HAVE PRODUCED THE CHANGES

Changes and progress have come about through three forces. Social and economic conditions of living have brought about a change in the legal problems and a subsequent realignment of the substantive law which relates to the rights of human beings under varying conditions; changes in the mechanics of trial procedure have brought a simplified process of enforcing these rights; and an open-minded attitude on the part of those in the legal profession has increasingly made the law a satisfactory tool for promoting the welfare of society. This last is illustrated by the activities of the American Bar Association and other legal groups.

PROGRESS IN THE FIELD OF CRIMINAL LAW

The field of criminal law procedure illustrates the second point. The attitude toward that particular subject is still one of inflexibility in many respects, as indicated by the lingering adherence to slow and unwieldy procedure with lengthy and verbose indictments, but these have to some extent been simplified. Usually the charge may be set forth by a brief statement of the facts, and it is possible in a large number of states for the prosecution to begin upon an information of the prosecuting officer instead of by means of the indictment of the grand jury. The difference between these two methods is important, for in the first instance the legally trained person is the one who finally determines whether or not a particular person shall be prosecuted, and in the second instance this is decided by the grand jury, which is made up of men who are without training or special knowledge of legal principles. The former way is simpler and more likely to expedite the trial process; therefore it is less expensive and is being used in many states in the trial of serious as well as minor crimes.

The process of growth has been at work in another way in the trial of cases, for in some states it is possible for a defendant to waive a jury trial and have a hearing before a judge. If this becomes a generally accepted practice the rules of evidence may become more flexible, as they are already in hearings before various commissions or boards of arbitration which serve in a combined administrative and judicial capacity. In order to avoid a trial, the court sometimes allows a defendant to compromise by pleading guilty to a lesser crime than the one with which he is charged. This is a step toward elimination of the delay which is so many times a part of the legal process, and it may be considered as one form of conciliation.

CONCILIATION

While delay may amount to a postponement of justice, a speedy course is often impossible under the present conditions except through conciliation. By this process the differences of the parties are settled by mutual and amicable agreement, in place of a battle in court which is fought by the attorneys for their clients and is expensive and time-consuming. The thing that is socially desirable but which cannot be accomplished by strict adherence to legal principles can sometimes be brought about by this practice, for the attorneys can often accomplish the desired result by applying the conference method in settling the client's difficulties. Conciliation is often used in family courts and has been effective in slander suits and even in cases involving disagreements on technical and scientific points. While it saves time and expense and transforms a disagreeable quarrel with its unpleasant aftermath into a friendly compromise, it also requires great skill, tact, and a singular understanding of human beings and their problems. Some legal authorities go so far as to say that an attempted conciliation should precede every litigation, and the American Bar Association endorses it by using the words of Lincoln as a preface to the canons of ethics of that association. "Discourage litigation. Persuade your neighbors to compromise whenever you can. Point out to them how the nominal winner is often the loser—in fees, expense, and waste of time. As a peacemaker the lawyer has a superior opportunity of being a good man."

LEGAL ORGANIZATIONS WORKING FOR JUSTICE

The legal aid societies which exist in our large cities bring help and justice to the clients who cannot afford to pay for legal services. The American Law Institute, an organization originated by some of the greatest legal personalities in the country, has worked since 1923 "to promote the clarification and simplification of the law and its better adaptation to social needs, to secure the better administration of justice, and to encourage and carry on scholarly and scientific legal work." One of its contributions has been a code that is recommended for criminal procedure. This provides the mechanics of trial procedure from the arrest through to the sentence and execution, and also the procedure on appeal. This is not a force to combat crime and its causes, neither does it change the personnel of those administering the law nor bring about the reformation or control of the offender after conviction. In these realms we are dealing with the unknown forces of the individual personality, the psychological and emotional life of individuals. However, the rather recent interest in prevention; the demand for better police personnel; and in some places the merger of inferior courts, such as police courts, with trial courts so that a single tribunal will be responsible for the whole procedure of examination and trial, show the results of the work done by this body.

INTERRELATIONSHIP WITH ALLIED FIELDS

The American Bar Association under its criminal law section has had committees on various subjects, and among the most important are those on medico-legal problems and on psychiatric jurisprudence. These committees have worked with committees from the American Medical Association and the American Psychiatric Association in an effort to understand the problems of criminal justice that show a close interrelationship with these allied fields. Along the line of research pertaining to mental disorders emphasis has been placed on four distinct stages. The first operates when a person is a mental defective and is taken into custody and given care for his own protection. The other three are effective after a criminal act has been committed, and relate to the condition of the person successively at the time the act was committed, at the time of trial, and, finally, at the time of the disposition of the party.

The science of human behavior, or psychiatry, has a bearing on all these points, and as early as 1929 this committee recommended the following:

"1. That there be available to every criminal and juvenile court a psychiatric service to assist the court in the disposition of offenders.

"2. That no criminal be sentenced for any felony in any case in which the judge has any discretion as to the sentence until there be filed as a part of the record a psychiatric report.

"3. That there be a psychiatric service available to every penal and correctional institution.

"4. That there be a psychiatric report on every prisoner convicted of a felony before he is released.

"5. That there be established in each state a complete system of administrative transfer and parole, and that there be no decision for or against any parole or any transfer from one institution to another, without a psychiatric report."

Later recommendations included a survey to ascertain the extent of psychiatric service in the courts. The problem of the petty offender who comes into the municipal or the police courts was studied in an effort to improve the methods in these courts by means of psychiatric case work. This would seem to indicate an interest in readjustment and unity within the profession of the law itself.

WHAT IS THE LAW?

The law must be considered as something more than rules of action written down in black and white which are interpreted by the legal profession. It deals not only with legal problems but also with all the problems of human relationships; it embodies ideals which are not based entirely upon legal precepts but upon tradition and centuries of living. These ideals form a pattern for life today. We find a group who would like to have the law more definite and exact in its answers, as a problem in mathematics; others complain of the rigidity and lack of creative insight. Both criticisms are partially true and though the law has a quality of definiteness in some of its terms and procedure, it can never be so fixed that it can settle any controversy that may arise in a way that is wholly predictable. It is this uncertainty that gives it life and fascination and which made Oliver Wendell Holmes, Jr., write: "When I think of the law I see a princess, mightier than she who once wrought a Bayeux, eternally weaving into her web dim figures of the ever lengthening past, figures too dim to be noticed by the idle, too symbolic to be interpreted by her pupils, but to the discerning eye disclosing every painful step and every world-shaking contest by which mankind has worked its way from savage isolation to organic social life."

SELECTED BIBLIOGRAPHY

ABBOTT, GRACE. *The Child and the State.* Chicago, 1938.

BRADWAY, JOHN S. *The Law and Social Work.* Chicago, 1929.

CLARK, WILLIAM LAWRENCE. *An Analytical Summary of American Law.* New York, 1923.

DEVINE, EDWARD T. *The Family and Social Work.* New York, 1912.

DOUGLAS, PAUL H. *Social Security in the United States.* New York, 1936.

GUILD, JANE PURCELL. *Living Within the Law.* New York, 1928.

HARPER, ROBERT FRANCIS. *The Code of Hammurabi.* Chicago, 1864.

LEVY, JOHN AND MUNROE, RUTH. *The Happy Family.* New York, 1938.

MAY, JOHN W. *May's Criminal Law.* Boston, 1905.

MCKELVIE, JOHN J. *Handbook of the Law of Evidence.* St. Paul, 1924.

POMEROY, JOHN N. *Equity Jurisprudence.* San Francisco, 1907.

POUND, ROSCOE. *The Spirit of the Common Law*. Boston, 1921.

RICHMOND, MARY E. *Social Diagnosis*. New York, 1917.

SMITH, R. H. *Justice and the Poor*. New York, 1924.

THOM, DOUGLAS A. *Normal Youth and Its Everyday Problems*. New York, 1932.

TURNER, FREDERICK JACKSON. *Frontiers in American History*. New York, 1921.

WILLOUGHBY, W. F. *Principles of Legislation, Organization, and Administration*. New York, 1934.

ZANE, JOHN M. *The Story of Law*. Garden City, N. Y., 1927.

Corpus Juris

National Reporter System.

Publications of the Child Welfare League of America.

Publications of the Federal Children's Bureau.

Publications of the National Child Labor Committee.

Publications of the Social Security Board.

Publications of the United States Bureau of Education.

Reports of the American Bar Association.

INDEX

www.ingramcontent.com/pod-product-compliance
Lightning Source LLC
LaVergne TN
LVHW090359210926
848480LV00002B/389
* 9 7 8 1 4 6 9 6 1 3 2 1 5 *